First published 1973 by Ernest Benn Limited
Sovereign Way, Tonbridge, Kent & 25 New Street Square, London, EC4A 2DL
© Jack Gibbs 1973
Distributed in Canada by
The General Publishing Company Limited, Toronto
Maps drawn by E. A. Chambers and K. Wass
Printed in Great Britain
ISBN 0 510–17809–x

*The illustration on the title page shows
the ruins of Guernica after the German bombing
in 1937*

CONTENTS

PRINCIPAL BOOKS CONSULTED

Spain 1808–1939, by Raymond Carr (Oxford)
La Révolution et la guerre d'Espagne, by P. Broué and E. Témime (Paris) – also available
    in an English translation
The Spanish Civil War, by Hugh Thomas (Penguin Books)
The Spanish Republic and the Civil War, 1931–1939, by G. Jackson (Princeton)
Politics and the Military in Modern Spain, by Stanley G. Payne (Stanford)

2   A street barricade in Barcelona, 1937

MAPS

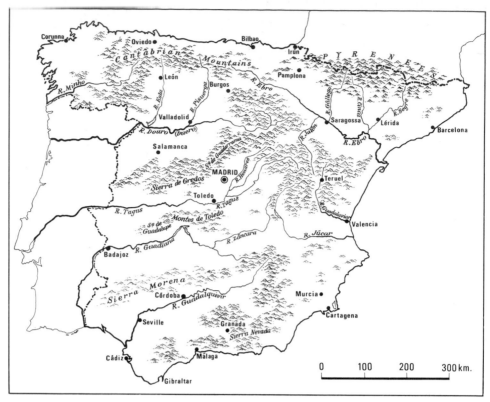

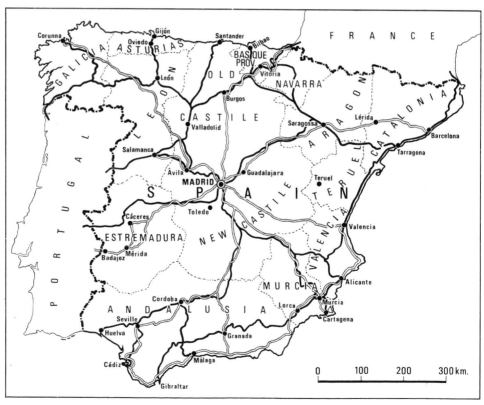

1 The Fermenting Bottle

WHEN FERNANDO VII lay dying in 1833, he is reported to have remarked that the cork was now removed from the fermenting bottle of Spain. He proved to be a good prophet, for civil war broke out almost at once over the succession. Fernando had ensured that his baby daughter, Isabel, would follow him on the throne, thus rejecting the claim of his brother Carlos that he was the rightful heir, being next in the male line. During Fernando's lifetime, Don Carlos had scrupulously refused to do more than put his case, but the Queen Mother, María Cristina, brought matters to a head by exiling him to Portugal. In November 1833 Don Carlos called on his supporters to resort to arms, and the First Carlist War broke out, to end after much bloodshed early in 1840. The main areas of Carlism were the Basque Provinces, Navarra, and parts of Aragón, Catalonia, and Valencia. After initial Carlist successes the war degenerated into a desultory struggle often marked by atrocities, and the bitterness it left behind was to develop into further risings in 1868 and 1872.

Carlism was only one of the numerous sources of division in Spain, and was essentially an internal dynastic struggle. Already, in Fernando's lifetime, other tensions had begun to make themselves felt and were to lead to much deeper and more threatening splits. The effects of the successful revolt of the English colonists in North America in 1776 and of the terrible events of the French revolution of 1789 were very soon noticeable in Spanish political life. In both these cases relatively untrained and ill-equipped men and women had overcome all organized forces used against them; in both cases a new type of state and government had emerged which appeared to mark a valuable advance on any previous system. Liberty and equality became the powerful new political slogans of the 1800s.

For any traditionally minded conservative Spaniard these two violent upheavals in the established order were ominous portents. It was not long before such fears became realities. Various efforts had been made to unite the Spanish Americas more closely to Spain, but events in Europe and in Spain itself had either caused the reforms to be abandoned or had made them ineffective. The move towards independence began in Venezuela in 1810 at Caracas, when the Town Council refused to recognize the Regency government of Spain, although it still proclaimed its loyalty to the new king, Fernando VII, who was actually firmly under Napoleon's control in France. However, there was stiff opposition by other colonists to this move, so the first stage of the movement was civil war. After many fluctuations, the rebels came out on top with the result that the first independent republic was set up in December 1819 under President Bolívar. It comprised the territory of Venezuela and New Granada, united as the republic of Colombia. By 1825 Spanish rule had ended everywhere from Mexico to Chile and Argentina; all that remained of Europe's largest modern empire was Cuba,

MAP 1a
Spain – Physical Features

MAP 1b
Spain – Provinces and Main Roads in 1936

Puerto Rico, and the Philippines. The blow to Spanish pride was overwhelming; almost equally damaging was the loss of export markets and raw materials. Henceforth Spain had to reconcile herself to being a third-class power, and she was to suffer further humiliation in 1898 when she lost her remaining territories in the New World, being forced to cede them to the United States when defeated by that nation.

Within Spain the new political ideas of the French revolution soon penetrated, and to counteract them censorship of literature from France was brought in in 1790, whilst efforts were made to save Louis XVI from execution. When the situation crystallized in May 1808 with the Madrid rising against the French occupying force, Spain was split into those traditionalists who resisted the invader in the name of patriotism, the more advanced Liberals who were Spaniards first and radicals afterwards, and the not inconsiderable group who considered that Spain could gain much by accepting French ideas on government (the *Afrancesados*). What was left of the Spanish government moved to Cadiz in 1810, where it was joined by any deputies who could get there. Most of these came from towns on the coast. As such places had been fertile areas for the propagation of more radical ideas, the dominant political colour of the Cadiz Cortes was liberal; this can be seen in the Constitution of 1812 which its members drew up. Though they suffered eclipse temporarily when the war ended and Fernando VII returned – some went to prison, others into exile – the Liberals came back into the picture again in due course. Up to the 1850s, there were three main political groups composed of numerous sub-groups of varying shades of opinion: Conservatives, Centre Party men, and Liberals. By the time the monarchy's status had

3   The Madrid Rising, when the Spanish unsuccessfully revolted against the occupying French forces; painted by Goya in *El dos de Mayo de 1808*

4   Don Carlos whose claim to the
Spanish throne caused civil war; after a
painting by López

5   Isabel II, Queen of Spain (1830–
1904) self-willed and lacking in diplomacy
she made the monarchy extremely unpopular

sunk under Isabel II's rule to its lowest level, a further group had appeared in the form
of a small number of Republicans.

Before considering the rise of further new political parties, something must now
be said of another factor which adds to the divisive elements in Spain. This is the
increasing intervention of the army in politics throughout the nineteenth and twentieth
centuries. Fernando VII had had to deal firmly with an attempt made in 1820 by an
army officer, Rafael Riego, to force a return to the Liberal Constitution of 1812. Riego
eventually received some popular support, but this first military *pronunciamiento* led
nowhere as the king soon succeeded in suppressing the revolt. In the reign of Isabel II
a General Espartero seized power in 1841, to be succeeded by two more generals,
Narváez and O'Donnell. Another officer, the Liberal General Prim, was responsible
for the rising which led to the queen's abdication in 1868, the actual manifesto being
issued by a navy man, Admiral Topete. In the confused situation of 1874 it was a group
of army officers who resolved the problems and it was General Martínez Campos
who proclaimed Alfonso king at Sagunto. Under Alfonso XIII the general strike of
1917 was broken largely by the army, which once more became a political influence,
this time representing popular feeling rather more accurately than the now discredited
politicians. Very soon the inept handling by the latter of the exhausting Moroccan war
opened the way to a military régime, so on 13 September 1923 Miguel Primo de Rivera
issued the usual manifesto and was entrusted with the formation of the Military
Directory which lasted until January 1930. The government of the country was run
very much like the command of an army, with ministers who were members of the

9

6 First Carlist War. Capture of Irún in 1837 by General Espartero and de Lacy Evans

7 General Prim; detail of a painting by Antonio María Esquivel

armed forces for most of the time. It did provide some stability for a period, but the solution of Spain's basic problems was quite beyond Primo de Rivera's abilities.

The army could not provide the inspiration needed to bind all Spaniards together; the monarch had lost his former powers and was fast becoming a constitutional head of state; could anything be effected by the third traditional pillar of the national life, the church?

The Spanish church, like the army, possesses a sharp sense of its identity, and, like the army, it is easily accused of being reactionary. But in both cases, this accusation is not always well founded. Some generals have been more liberal than the governments they were trying to bring down. The church has frequently advocated the need for social improvements, and the poorer parish clergy differed but little from their parishioners in outlook. This paradoxical combination of apparent opposites is a feature of the church in Spain, and can be traced back a long way in time. In the sixteenth century, the church was the one unifying institution that held power equally over the whole of the country. The king had to take care to appease local feelings, and had to consider the attitude of the local parliaments and courts. The Archbishop of Toledo and the Inquisitor-General had no such problems. Decisions made by them were binding everywhere automatically.

In addition to providing this strong territorial link, the church's scholars also created a firm social unity. In the first half of the sixteenth century, they paid considerable attention to the subject of the individual's duties and rights in society, often coming to unexpectedly egalitarian conclusions. It was as if an attempt was being made to show that as all men were equal in the sight of God, they should be equal in the sight of each other. But under the threatening pressure of the Reformation, these democratic ideas began to wither. It became dangerous to speculate or to criticize, so a decline in original intellectual activity set in. By the early nineteenth century, the church was the main resistance to the new liberal ideas. In 1837 the Liberals retaliated by cutting down the church's holdings of land, thus weakening its grip on the lower classes. In spite of a revival some fifty years later, accompanied by increasing participation in business and investment, the church faced a steady decline in regular worshippers. Its influence was still strong as it provided much of the school-teaching up to 1931, though the universities, once a clerical stronghold, had been secularized by the Liberals.

In more recent years, it almost looks as if the early fervour and enthusiasm shown by the mass of Spanish Catholics 400 years ago faded as the church failed to complete the task of unifying the nation, only to be transferred, as it were, to the newer 'religions' of Socialism, Anarchism, and Communism. All these creeds are just as sure that they each provide the sole organization capable of uniting all men as brothers. Under their competitive influence the Spanish church in the 1930s began to regain something of its former position. As its power decreased its spiritual quality seems to have risen, and once again great scholars and saintly men appear at the highest level. Cardinal Segura, the Primate of Spain, demonstrates in his life many of the qualities of Spanish Catholicism. An implacable opponent of all heresies, he began his priesthood in the most backward part of Spain where he became known as a humanitarian reformer. When

8   The proclamation in Madrid of the Provisional Government of 1868

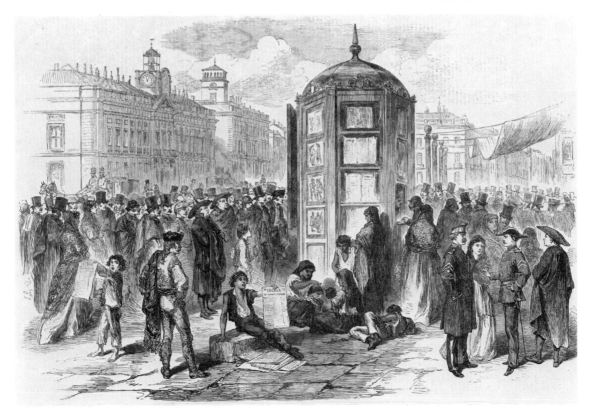

9   The Archbishop of Granada denouncing the First
Republic in a sermon in 1873

he rose to the Primacy at the age of forty-six, he continued to live the simplest of lives
and worked as hard as his parish priests. He combined this spiritual vigour with the
highest scholarship. As a student at college, he had been awarded three doctorates.

10   [*opposite*] Armed 'Home Guards' in the 1909 revolution

2 Watertight Compartments

TWO NEW POLITICAL GROUPS which had their origins abroad, and which took root in Spain during the reign of Amadeo (1871–3), were basically revolutionary so that one effect of their growth was to intensify and make more rigid the country's divisions. The first was Socialism, developed largely from the theories of Karl Marx; the second was Anarchism which grew from the ideas of the Russian revolutionary, Bakunin. In 1871 the Marxist cause had been championed by Pablo Iglesias, who with some like-minded radicals formed a small group. In 1872 they founded the first Spanish Socialist Party, which Iglesias led until his death in 1925. They set up a trade union, the Unión General de Trabajadores, to promote their ideals. It was a small organization with most of its members in Madrid, Asturias, and Bilbao. The union became interested in workers' education, an interest which led to the opening of *casas del pueblo* in towns of all sizes. These combined the local headquarters with a library and café, and attracted new members, so that by the end of World War I the membership had reached some 200,000, and there were a few deputies in the Cortes.

Pablo Iglesias was followed by Largo Caballero, a popular man with the workers, who was to become the first Labour Minister of the republic in 1931. With him in the Cabinet was another Socialist, Indalecio Prieto, who was an unsuccessful Minister of Finance. These two men were the representatives of the two sides of the party. Largo Caballero was the honest trade union official who backed the forces of disciplined, reasonable, workers in their attempts to better conditions and who was 'one of them' – he was a building worker who had risen by his own hard work and integrity. Prieto was an eloquent speaker whose quick wits had made him rich and who was the favourite of the middle class supporters of the Socialists. He found no difficulty in combining his reformist ideas with his membership of the Madrid Ateneo, the Liberal centre of arts and letters. The two leaders were incompatible almost from the start so that the Socialists began to fall into two main groups, one of workers whose hero was Largo Caballero, and one of middle class or professional people around Prieto. The first

11　Artist's impression of an incident in Granada in the 1901 riots, as an arms depot is stormed

12　The scene in the Calle Mayor in Madrid after the attempt on

group began to move towards a more extreme and revolutionary position after 1933 as Largo Caballero decided to meet the Anarchists' challenge by breaking with the middle class parties and, outwardly at least, moving the Socialist Party to the left. The Socialist Union, the U.G.T., thus became the militant defence against the power of the Anarchist Union (the Confederación Nacional de Trabajo), and inter-union conflict was bound to ensue sooner or later to introduce a further divisive element into Republican solidarity.

The Anarchists also began in a very small way in 1868 when Giuseppe Fanelli came to Spain from Italy to spread the ideas of Mikhail Bakunin. This was the year of the final collapse of the absolute monarchy when the traditional type of state, with its dependence on law and discipline imposed from without, was partially discredited. It is therefore no surprise that Bakunin's theory of anarchy (meaning 'no government') was looked upon as a revelation in certain circles. Society was to be made up of large numbers of groups or corporations, each self-governing and covering a social group (municipality), a particular profession, a trade, and so on. These corporations would form links with each other as necessary, thus creating a unified society composed of living cells of varying types and sizes. Punishment for any disturbance of this order would be by public disapproval of the individual concerned. Justice for all would be thus ensured by criminals being censured instead of imprisoned. This attempt to bring society back to the Golden Age was in line with the longings of some Spaniards for that

14

Alfonso XIII's life at his wedding in 1906

13 Artist's impression of an Anarchist bomb exploding in Barcelona in 1905

distant legendary past when the village or town was supposed to have been a sturdily independent and close-knit group, and when guilds and trade corporations were valued organizations; a period of benevolence and mutual brotherhood.

The first development of Fanelli's visit was to be found in Andalusia, an area of poor farm labourers and workers, and the early Anarchists went from village to village, preaching the virtues of self-control, vegetarianism, fidelity, and co-operation. They also taught the illiterate to read and write. One effect of this was the implanting of the belief that as the political system was so oppressive, it would have to be destroyed before the brave new world could be created. The First Republic took fright, suppressing all forms of Anarchism in 1872, but not before a small band of determined men had seized Alcoy after a strike and had slaughtered the mayor and the local Civil Guards. Similar violent acts mark the history of Spanish Anarchism which soon spread from Andalusia to Barcelona, a city which had attracted many Andalusians, who had gone there to benefit by the vast industrial growth which was a source of work. Terrorism grew and with it so did repression. The Prime Minister, Cánovas del Castillo, was killed as were two other Premiers later. An Anarchist bomb was thrown at Alfonso XIII on his wedding day. In 1909 Barcelona experienced violent riots in the *Semana Trágica*. Then in 1911 an Anarchist labour union was formed in the shape of the Confederación Nacional de Trabajo, which had well over half a million members by the end of World War I. The political struggle in Barcelona took on the worst features of gang

15

warfare as Anarchist morale was raised by the successful example of the Bolshevik revolution in Russia.

Primo de Rivera succeeded in controlling the movement for a time by energetic action, which drove some of the more militant Anarchists abroad. Men like Buenaventura Durruti based themselves in France, from time to time making commando-type raids into Spain. In one such attack in 1923 the Archbishop of Saragossa was murdered. A meeting was held in Valencia in 1927 to form a suitable body to plan extreme militant action. The outcome was the Federación Anarquista Ibérica whose revolutionary fervour brought it into conflict with a large section of the C.N.T. This was divided by now into two main groups, one in Barcelona with its adoption of the theory of Syndicalism based on factory syndicates as the cell units, and the Andalusians who adopted the self-sufficient *pueblo* (village or town) as their cell unit.

Up to 1920, the Anarchists and Socialists thus comprised by far the largest section of the Left Wing in Spanish politics. Then in that year a third party was born in the shape of the Spanish Communist Party (Partido Comunista Español) set up by dissatisfied members of the Socialist Youth committee. As the Socialists themselves were not unsympathetic to much that the Soviet Union had done, this new group did not find much support at first. In fact, a second Communist Party appeared in 1921 formed by those who wanted to join the Third International (the *terceristas*). This party was the Partido Comunista Obrero de España. Under orders from Moscow in 1922 the two groups were again combined into one.

14 The popular idea of an Anarchist making bombs in his garret (1906 period). His tools had to be fairly simple because expensive materials would have aroused suspicion

15 Damage in Barcelona during the rising of 1909

16 Buenaventura Durruti, the Anarchist leader. He was eventually killed in street fighting in Madrid, November 1936

Up to 1931 the history of the party is largely one of attempted agitation and firm government repression, of argument over policy, and of a lack of consistent leadership. Most of the original membership had come from the Asturian miners and the iron workers of Bilbao, though it did get an unexpected windfall in 1927 in Seville when some C.N.T. leaders came over and there was a consequent increase in support from the city's working class. But basically morale was not high so that total membership in 1931 was very low still. When the Comintern began to build up a Popular Front against Fascism in 1934, the Communist Party took its place in the alliance, very far to the left as a result of Largo Caballero's own move leftwards with the Socialists. In fact, the Spanish Party was forced to adopt a more extreme position than the Soviet Union desired. When the Civil War did break out, the Communists were therefore the farthest left of all and very ready to seize power if the opportunity came by reason of any failure of either of the other radical groups to pursue the war effectively.

However, not all those who had been attracted to Soviet Communism remained firm Communists. In 1931 two men broke away from the rigid party line. One was Andrés Nin, who had spent a long period in Russia and who could not accept Stalin's violent attack on Trotsky. He formed the Oposición Comunista more or less on vaguely Trotskyist lines. His comrade, Joaquín Maurín, founded a somewhat similar party at the same time in the Bloque Obrero y Campesino (B.O.C.). The two splinter parties merged into one in mid-1936 to become the Partido Obrero de Unificación Marxista (P.O.U.M.) with most of their strength in Catalonia and Madrid.

One point of interest in the history of Spanish Communism underlines the difficulties which beset political parties in their search for overall unity. In 1933 the Communists had to resign themselves to setting up a Catalan section to overcome the reluctance of Catalans to being associated with a *Spanish* group. This was the Partit Comunista de Catalunya. Regional patriotism is a factor to be reckoned with even today, just as it has been for 2,000 years or more. The Romans had divided Spain into three provinces, each comprising a large number of regional assize areas. The Visigoths had failed in the task of unification though they had managed to enforce one religion and one legal code over much of the peninsula. When the slow reconquest of the country began after the Muslim invasion of 711, it was based on widely separated and completely uncoordinated areas, so that after a century or so Christian Spain was in reality eight kingdoms or counties. Eventual fusion of certain areas left three blocs, reduced to two under the Catholic monarchs, Ferdinand and Isabel, and then briefly to one under Philip II and Philip III. But the peninsula was never really a united and homogeneous state even then. Certain areas retained a very strong sense of their individual identity in spite of heavy centralizing pressures, and separatism has always been a possibility. Regional patriotism has forced even the most monolithic of parties to adapt itself to local feelings.

The two most important potentially separatist zones are the Basque Provinces and Catalonia, and both achieved their own governments during the war. But Galicia, Aragón, Valencia, Andalusia, and even Castile have been affected by similar movements towards some form of autonomy or partial self-government. The problem of how to direct what could be dangerous tendencies towards national disintegration was one that the early Republican politicians recognized in the previous century as far back as 1868 when the First Republic came into existence. Their solution was Federalism, by which Spain would be divided into a number of viable provinces, each with limited self-government. Little attention was paid to the economic difficulties which this would have led to, and the republic fell before the theory was put to the test.

In Castile and Valencia, there was little real support for any form of separatism or federalism, but Andalusia did see one attempt in February 1933 when a Regional Assembly met at Córdoba. The resultant arguments and heated discussions led nowhere. Aragón, which had retained its own Cortes and privileges for a long period after union with Castile, had an autonomist group of no great importance. Of the other three, Galicia had an Autonomist Party based on a movement going back to the end of the nineteenth century. A draft Statute was prepared and had been passed by the various local town councils by December 1932, but the fall of the government in Madrid put an end to further action.

In Catalonia, the situation was more complex in some ways. After the failure of the revolt of 1640 and of a similar rising against the first Bourbon king, Philip V, in 1714, the Catalans had been firmly held in subjection. But they had not forgotten their past history and a literary renaissance which can be dated from 1833 brought with it a political reawakening. At the end of the century a Right Wing party, largely composed of wealthier businessmen and some intellectuals, had been created in the Lliga Catalana. In 1913 limited self-government was granted by Madrid, a move which led to further growth in political life such as the foundation of another party, Acció Catalana. However Primo de Rivera stamped out all forms of Catalanism in 1923 and it went underground until his fall.

Once more the Catalans began to press their claims, a new group now having been formed by an amalgamation of Acció Catalana and two or three other small radical parties. This was the Esquerra Catalana (Catalan Left), mostly consisting of small traders and shopkeepers at first. When the king left Spain in April 1931, it was Colonel Francisco Macià, leader of Esquerra, who proclaimed a Catalan republic, supported by

Lluis Companys, his second-in-command. The Madrid Republican government at once persuaded them to replace the words 'Estat Català' by the less obviously separatist title of 'Generalitat', the old traditional name. Eventually a Statute of Autonomy passed the Cortes on 9 September 1932 after it had suffered some drastic amendments made to placate those who claimed it was going to give Catalonia complete independence. Then in October 1934, during a general strike called against the new government of Alejandro Lerroux, widespread unrest throughout Spain was suddenly turned into violence by Companys who, on 6 October, announced the support of Catalonia for all now fighting against the new reactionary government. The rebellion lasted twelve hours, ending in the surrender of the rebels and the withdrawal of the Statute of Autonomy. In March 1936, one of Premier Azaña's first acts was to reverse this decision, so that Catalonia once more had its own government.

The Basque Provinces of Álava, Guipúzcoa, and Vizcaya, and the Basques of Navarra are the most profoundly nationalist of all in that the effect of their unique language and deep consciousness of their closely-knit social and racial group have enabled them to retain a sense of identity. For many centuries they have fiercely defended their special rights (*fueros*) and have remembered proudly that they were never conquered by the Muslim invaders of 711. Their assembly, held every second year at the famous oak tree of Guernica, has its origins far back in the Middle Ages or

17 The Barcelona bus depot under police guard during the 1934 strikes

18 The radical leader Alejandro Lerroux

earlier, and at it the Basques would receive the king's oath to respect their rights and would elect their own council. They are ardently Roman Catholic, opposing any form of Liberalism in the early nineteenth century, and they provided most of the Carlist forces in 1833, as the result of which their *fueros* were all abolished in 1839. The effect of this disaster was to reinforce their determination to preserve their identity. In 1931 the Provinces refused to support any anti-clerical measures of the republic, and the leader of the Basque Nationalists, José Antonio Aguirre, was even approached by General Orgaz and the Monarchists who sought support for any possible move to overthrow the régime. Aguirre would have none of this, preferring to go his own way alone. In June 1932, representatives of the Provinces and of Navarra met to vote on a draft Statute of Autonomy. Navarra turned it down (123 to 109), the other delegates giving it overwhelming support (245 to 14). Unfortunately for the Basques, the Statute ran into a series of delays in the Cortes and was only passed in October 1936 when the Basque Republic (Euzkadi) was set up as an autonomous area with Aguirre as President.

It is clear that up to 1931 Spain was falling apart into a multiplicity of social and political groups, some large, others small, but all determined to achieve their particular objective. Violent clashes, widespread unrest, strikes, and economic disruption were inevitable, as was equally violent repression. For some, a military dictatorship was the only effective solution, for others the logical step was a revolution inspired by the Left which would destroy the so-called enemies of progress. The Second Republic appeared to provide some basis for hope that at last the fragmented country would become one state, but it soon became obvious that the old divisions within and between classes and

19   The Council Chamber at Guernica during the Basque
Republic Presidential Election in 1936

20   The Basque Nationalist leader President José Aguirre

21   Part of the crowd of 500,000 'Free and Autonomous' Catalonians demonstrating against Fascism in Barcelona, 1934

parties were still vigorous. Quite a number of the republic's earlier supporters became disillusioned as time went on. The new state was not what they had envisaged – the age of the Brotherhood of Man was still a long way in the future. It is no surprise therefore that in one of the slogans of the Right Wing – 'España, una, grande, libre' – the emphasis is on *una*. Without unity nothing could be achieved.

But the old parties of the Right were no more successful than the newer groups of the Left in providing the governments and policies which could command the respect and co-operation of all Spaniards. The defeat of 1898 and the long-drawn-out Moroccan war led to increasing public distaste for most of the professional politicians. This decline was hastened by the splits which had developed in the main parties, the Conservatives and the Liberals, both of which had divided into three in the early twentieth century with roughly the same pattern of right, centre, and left wings. There was no real driving force in either party to inspire the mass of Spaniards to regain their trust in parliamentary institutions. In addition, there were the Monarchists supporting Alfonso XIII, and the Carlists who looked for a king from the other branch of the family. The latter were singleminded, deeply religious, but of no political weight, as their desire to see Spain return to traditional forms of government had little relevance to the actual state of the country. Certainly up to 1931 the Right Wing and Liberal politicians had little to offer to counter the vigorous activity of the Left Wing. The temptation of men like Primo de Rivera to revive Spain's national life by resorting to more forceful and less constitutional methods is therefore understandable.

The growing tensions and pressures of the pre-Civil War period highlight very clearly the basic social and political divisions of Spain, with all their potential dangers.

Fernando VII had not been far out in his death-bed prophecy. And back in 1921, the philosopher José Ortega y Gasset made the same point in his *España Invertebrada* when he wrote: 'Hoy es España, más bien que una nación, una serie de compartimientos'. It was beyond doubt ten years later that Spain was indeed a series of watertight compartments.

22 General Primo de Rivera and his cabinet of 1924

3 The Spanish Fury

'THE SPANISH FURY' – 'la furia española' – was an apt phrase to describe the irresistible onrush of sixteenth-century Spanish infantry and their equally violent treatment of the civilian population of the countries they conquered or on whom they were billeted. At its best, it denotes a bravery and endurance beyond the normal; at its worst, a blind urge to annihilate all opposition. In modern political life, Spaniards of passionate and deep convictions have tended to give expression to their fury in violent words rather than actions, but when tempers get too hot and the individual really sees himself threatened by more than speeches, his reaction is sharp and often bloody. The one possible solution is kill or be killed. Up to 1931 there had been numerous clashes which had led to fierce and pitiless fighting, such as the Carlist wars, risings against the government, political riots, and so on. But none of these had developed into a full-scale civil war involving the whole country directly. Then suddenly in early 1931, such a civil war appeared imminent.

For some years before that date, Alfonso XIII had been losing the support of certain of his people. Frequent changes in the government had forced him to use his executive powers to keep the state going, and he tried to stabilize the position by balancing one political group against another. A more subtle man could have succeeded in this dangerous procedure, but Alfonso did not possess the necessary political skill. He was accused by the Republican Socialists of playing politics, of acting unconstitutionally. As a result his position was being slowly undermined in spite of his apparent popularity. During the last half of 1930, a number of general strikes occurred and there were student riots in the universities. A Revolutionary Committee led by Niceto Alcalá Zamora, a progressive Catholic, was formed and planned to open its campaign against the government on 15 December, but was forestalled by a mutiny of the Jaca garrison. The mutineers proclaimed a republic and moved towards Huesca to spread the rising. They were overwhelmed, their leaders, Captain Fermín Galán and Captain Ángel García Hernández, being shot. The rumour went round that Alfonso had prevented his ministers from showing any leniency. Instead of going ahead with plans for its own attack, the Revolutionary Committee issued a manifesto and assumed the rôle of the Provisional Government of the Republic. Those signatories who could be found were promptly arrested.

The next significant step was another manifesto, signed this time by three leading men, Doctor Gregorio Marañón, a famous specialist, José Ortega y Gasset the philosopher, and Ramón Perez de Ayala the novelist. This foretold the impending collapse of the monarchy and called for the collaboration of all intellectuals, professional men, lawyers, and young people to welcome the coming republic. On 14 February the government resigned in the face of the deteriorating national situation. Admiral Juan B. Aznar became Premier, and the new cabinet at once announced that municipal elections would be held shortly on Sunday 12 April. Before that date sentence was passed on the Revolutionary Committee members on trial, each being given six months and one day. Next day they all had their sentences remitted and left prison to the cheers of thousands of their supporters. The elections passed off quietly, most politicians expecting

23 Alfonso XIII and
his eldest son Prince Juan

24 Proclamation of the
Republic by Colonel Macià
in Barcelona, April 1931

25 Alcalá Zamora, first
president of the Republic

that the results would show a marked Republican gain but no more. Monday in
Spain was and is a day with no newspapers beyond a news-sheet. The first results to be
made known were largely rural ones, with the Monarchists leading by over three seats
to one. But as the city results came through, the Republican majorities were seen to be
enormous. Spain was becoming a republic in a day. For Alfonso XIII the moment was
one of danger and tragedy, for over the whole country there was an almost equal
division of pro- and anti-Monarchist votes. Alcalá Zamora had given him until sunset
to decide on his next step. If he stayed, civil war was inevitable, but if he left Spain, he
was abandoning his position as king. He made the wise choice and prepared to depart.
That evening Spain was a republic. The next day, 15 April, the Revolutionary Committee became the Provisional Government. It proceeded to demonstrate its confidence by publishing Alfonso's final dignified statement to his people.

For just under a month all went well. The Monarchists seemed to be stunned into
inactivity by the king's departure, whilst the church appeared to be waiting to see what
was going to happen. The Provisional Government took over the task of ruling in a
smooth and efficient manner. But then the publication by the Monarchist paper *A.B.C.*
of an interview with Alfonso and the appearance of a pastoral letter from the Cardinal
Archbishop of Toledo, Doctor Pedro Segura, attacking the destroyers of religion,
sparked off five days of violence. The *A.B.C.* offices in Madrid were burned out as were
a number of churches, convents, and monasteries, and Cardinal Segura had to leave
Spain. The violence spread only to Andalusia but there much destruction was done
and martial law had to be declared. Suddenly, all was quiet again as stern measures
were taken to control the rioting. To meet any further trouble the government

strengthened the para-military Civil Guard and formed a corps of *Guardias de Asalto* or Shock Troops. But relations with the church had become even more strained, especially as some degree of secularization had already been introduced together with freedom of worship.

Elections for the Cortes were held in June, the results being as follows:

Right Wing	Monarchists Conservatives Others	1- 19 40	= 60
Centre	Right Wing Republicans	30	= 30
Left	Republican Alliance Socialists Radical Socialists	120 116 60	= 296
	Esquerra and Galicians	59	= 59

The massive support for Republicanism was not however enough for the more extreme element. The Syndicalists and Communists started a series of disturbances which culminated in a general strike in Seville on 20 July. The government's reaction was swift and determined and order was restored. The government could now turn its attention to debating the new Constitution. The discussions covered some five months, the final version being ratified on 9 December 1931.

The Constitution began by declaring the principles of liberty, justice, and equality on which the new state was to be based. It then dealt with general organization. All the existing local government system was to be retained, but any area desiring and ready for self-government could ask for the grant of a Statute of Autonomy. Under the

26　The Second Republic 1931. Scene in the Puerta del Sol in Madrid as the Flag of the Republic is carried in triumph through the streets in an open car, 1931

heading of political and individual guarantees, provision was made for the abolition of noble titles and of all special privileges. Complete freedom of expression of opinion was allowed. Women were given the vote, and the age of enfranchisement was fixed at twenty-three. Freedom of conscience was guaranteed, and the Catholic Church ceased to be the official church of Spain. By 1933 payment of the clergy out of state funds was to cease. Any religious order owing obedience outside the state was to be disbanded, and no order must engage in public education. Then came a section on marriage, both civil marriage and divorce being permitted. Education became compulsory and wholly secular. With regard to legislation, there was to be a Cortes consisting of a single Chamber and elected for four years. There was to be a President chosen by an Electoral College and holding office for six years. He was to nominate the Prime Minister and might suspend or dissolve the Cortes, though if he did so new elections must be held within sixty days. Such dissolution could only be authorized twice during his term of office. Laws were normally to be promulgated within fifteen days unless declared to be urgent, when promulgation was immediate. A non-urgent law could be sent back by the President and must then gain a two-thirds majority to be promulgated. The Constitution as a whole was designed to provide a working document which would satisfy most people though it contained some potentially dangerous provisions, as, for example, the articles concerning the church, which were clearly full of pitfalls.

It was in fact the anti-clerical section of the Constitution which led to the first signs of trouble when it came before the Cortes on 8 October. Azaña spoke vigorously and at length against Spanish Catholicism, and the articles were passed, but not before the Prime Minister, Alcalá Zamora, had resigned on 14 October and had been replaced by Azaña himself. The new Premier then took steps to block any attempt by Alcalá Zamora to stiffen Catholic opposition in the Cortes by planning the effective neutralization of his opponent. On 9 December a large majority of the Cortes voted the former Prime Minister into the Presidency. The next day he took the oath of office, and two days after that, the Papal Nuncio had the ironically fitting task of reading an address of congratulation to him on behalf of the Diplomatic Corps. He had already seen severe limitations imposed on the activity of the Spanish church, and now the Jesuit order was marked down for dissolution and expulsion. Just over a month later, in fact, the decree dated 23 January 1932 was signed giving the order just over a week to close down its religious houses and schools before the property was to be taken over and its members were to leave the country.

The autumn of 1931 had seen other sensational events. A drastic Law for the Defence of the Republic, introduced by Azaña, had been passed almost on the nod a week after he assumed power. By it the Home Secretary had the personal power to act against everything from riots to damaging rumours. The dangers inherent in such a measure were only too obvious so that attacks on its provisions were widespread, though the law remained in force until the end of July 1933, when it was replaced by a more reasonable Law of Public Order. The second event was the trial in absence of Alfonso XIII before the Cortes for crimes against the state. The king was judged to be guilty of high treason and banished in perpetuity. Otherwise, apart from a Cabinet reshuffle when Alejandro Lerroux and the Radicals left the government, the year ended quietly.

The year 1932 began tragically. On 31 December 1931, at Castilblanco in the province of Badajoz, a clash occurred between the villagers and the Civil Guard. A

27 The 1933 Troubles. Wreckage of the Barcelona–
Seville express after a bridge was blown near Valencia.
Thirty-nine people were killed and many more injured

proposed political meeting had been banned, but the ban was ignored. The Civil Guard
then intervened, four of them being murdered by being knifed and battered to death.
Immediately the government's enemies struck. In an unexpected alliance, Syndicalists,
Anarchists, and Communists stirred up riots, the main centres being Bilbao and
Valencia. A full revolt broke out in upper Catalonia in the Llobregat valley, but was at
once crushed. Azaña was a vigorous opponent of all who tried to use violence against
him.

Once more Spain quietened down, so that the Cortes could turn its attention to
solving a particularly urgent problem, that of the poverty-stricken and hopeless con-
dition of the peasantry in the south, where farm workers spent their lives toiling in
wretched conditions on the huge estates or *latifundios* of Extremadura and Andalusia.
Not unexpectedly, the Syndicalists and other extreme groups had seized on this as a
political weapon, so the government had to act firmly. It began to debate a draft
Agrarian Law under which all estates over a certain size would be expropriated and
the owners indemnified according to the value they themselves had placed on the
land for tax assessment purposes – a scheme which was not at all to the liking of the
owners! The areas thus taken over were to be distributed amongst the peasants who
worked them. The law was passed in September, but its administration ran into

difficulties, so vast was the problem. The only other major piece of legislation was the passing of the Catalan Statute of Autonomy on 9 September.

But, shortly before this, the relative calm had been broken by an outbreak of activity from an unexpected quarter. Previously any attempt at armed risings had been inspired by the extremists of the Left Wing. But on 10 August one of the traditional pronunciamiento-type revolts occurred when a Monarchist group of nobles and ex-army officers rose in Madrid against the new republic. As a pending revolt had been café gossip for days Azaña was ready and had no difficulty in repressing it. Another rising timed to start in Seville at the same moment was led by the Director-General of the Civil Guard, General Sanjurjo, but his rebellion also failed thanks to prompt steps taken by the Civil Guard themselves and by the reinforcements sent to the area. He was arrested, and sentenced to death, the sentence being commuted to life imprisonment. He was reprieved under the Amnesty Law of 1933 and returned to become the possible leader of the 1936 rising, only to be killed taking off from Portugal for Spain. His action in 1932 may have been taken on his own responsibility as he was a somewhat flamboyant man. It is suggested that his plane crashed because it was overloaded by the weight of his luggage and so hit the top of a tree!

This abortive attempt must have shown the men who were in fact already plan-

28   Cartoons from the Rightist satirical magazine *Gracia y Justicia* of May 1932. (*Left to right*) Lerroux (the historic republican waiting for Azaña's majority to dissolve); Azaña (Minister of War as well as Prime Minister); Prieto (Minister of Public Works and Socialist leader); Galarza (Director General of Security); Largo Caballero Minister of Labour and Socialist Trade Union leader); Macià (President of the Generalitat).

ning a Right Wing revolt that it was still far too soon to translate plans into action. Already in May 1931 a small group had begun to meet under the title of the Independent Monarchist Club. The meetings were led by two generals, Orgaz and Ponte, and had attracted a leading Monarchist, the journalist and writer, Ramiro de Maeztu, who was later executed by the Republicans. The original plans were to found a quite legal Monarchist party called Renovación Española, issue a publication entitled *Acción Española* to encourage attacks on the Republic, and set up an underground group in the form of a Unión Militar Española to attract dissident officers. They had little doubt that this last organization would prosper as Azaña had permitted any officers who felt they could not swear an oath of allegiance to the new state to retire without losing their pay in a decree of 23 April 1931. There were thus quite a few officers who did not support the republic and who had time on their hands which they could very well employ in building up the U.M.E. Such men would also appreciate the importance of discipline and sound planning, both essential requirements if any plot was to have a chance of success. It might be a matter of years before the right moment presented itself.

One result of the revolt of 10 August 1932 was that, though it had collapsed, it had indirectly helped the rebels' cause. In addition to sentencing the culprits to imprisonment, the government confiscated their property. This harsh attitude was responsible for turning quite a number of non-political Spaniards against the government. By taking the revolt too seriously Azaña had unwittingly helped the cause of those enemies on the Right who were working for the overthrow of the republic.

A second revolt, this time organized by the Communists, occurred in September and was crushed in its turn.

In October 1932 the debate began in the Cortes on the Law of Confessions and Congregations, designed to complete the legislation drastically limiting the church's power and that of the religious orders, who were to give up all teaching by 31 December 1933. This last point seemed to many to be unwise as some 7,000 new schools and a corresponding number of new teachers would be needed to replace the religious school system. The Opposition used the debates to obstruct the government so that the law was only signed by Alcalá Zamora after much hesitation on 2 June 1933, seven months later.

Azaña had begun to lose control by the beginning of 1933. In early January, Anarchist revolts took place in Madrid, Barcelona, Lérida, Seville, and Valencia, but once more were suppressed quickly. Then, at the same time, a much more damaging riot took place at the village of Casas Viejas, near Medina de Sidonia. A group of Anarchists from outside the area proclaimed a Communistic type of local government there on 11 January. At once the Civil Guard and the Shock Troops moved in, but suffered heavy losses. Orders came from Madrid that no quarter was to be given, and the last of the rebels, his daughter, and six others were burned to death when the troops set their house on fire. Azaña was furiously attacked in the Cortes, only winning the division by forty-three votes.

The growing unpopularity of his government was again shown in the results of the partial municipal elections held on 23 April. Government candidates won just over 5,000 seats, but the Right was close behind them with about 5,000, whilst the Centre and Left Opposition parties reached 4,300. A wave of strikes and riots followed, so Azaña resigned on 9 June. As no one could be found to follow him, he came back for a further three months until again he had to resign in face of the growing difficulties in controlling

29

29　President Zamora casts his vote in the November elections, 1933

30　The 1933 elections. A Madrid queue at a polling station showing women voting for the first time

the Cortes. Elections were arranged for 19 November, and the results showed a significant swing as follows:

Right Wing parties 207 (+165)
Centre parties　　　167 (+ 31)
Left Wing parties　　99 (−192)

It was now clear that Spain was moving to the Right once more.

One reason for this important development was certainly the effect of the formation of a coalition of the parties of the Right in the Confederación Española de Derechas Autónomas, which now formed the largest bloc in the Cortes and in which the Acción Popular group was now a powerful influence with sixty-two deputies. The C.E.D.A. leader was José María Gil Robles, a young man who had been much impressed by Hitler, whom he met in 1933. Like the German Führer, Gil Robles was careful to attract middle class support, but, as he had to keep together a somewhat motley group of other supporters too, his political ideas were not too precise. Unlike Hitler, he thus provided little inspiration for the younger generation, some of whom began to turn to other new parties, whose political philosophy was based on Fascism and National Socialism.

The career of Benito Mussolini, who had taken over power in Italy in 1922, attracted some to advocate a Fascist solution with its firm centralized government and its apparently progressive social legislation. Fascism had also shown how Communist and extreme Socialist activities could be effectively curbed by force, an example well calculated to appeal to those Spaniards who regarded any Left Wing supporters as dangerous and potentially violent revolutionaries. Ernesto Giménez Caballero had been the founder of Spanish Fascism in 1928, with a fiery political creed which was based on reversing the decline in prestige of the Mediterranean countries, especially those who owed their origin to Imperial Rome.

The starting point of another and similar movement was Germany, where Adolf Hitler's theories of National Socialism were gaining ground. In 1931 the basic ideas of the Nazis were publicly expounded in Spain by Ramiro Ledesma Ramos, whose admiration for Hitler was such that he adopted the same hair style. A militant and responsible discipline was to be the key to everything. In the same year a native of Valladolid, Onésimo Redondo, began to put forward very similar ideas, having been much impressed by what he had seen of the Nazi movement in Germany. He and Ledesma then came together to found a suitable organization to advance their views – the Juntas de Ofensiva Nacional-Sindicalista (J.O.N.S.). This declared against separatism and class struggles, and advocated the recapture of Gibraltar and the strengthening of Spain's position in Morocco. For a year or two this group was small in numbers, without the funds to do more than keep in existence, but with a certain proportion of fanatical members who could easily cause considerable trouble.

Whilst Redondo and Ledesma were trying to build up the J.O.N.S., the son of the late General Primo de Rivera was attracting the attention of the younger Fascists in Spain. José Antonio Primo de Rivera, Marqués de Estella, had begun his political life as a Monarchist and Catholic. He was an eloquent speaker whose ideas developed towards the formulation of a political theory based on national unity and class co-operation, which would avoid the illogical confusion of much Liberal thinking and the

31   Catalonia. A column of the semi-Fascist *Escamots* of José Dencás marching through the Exhibition Grounds in Barcelona, 1934

violence of revolutionary Socialism. Like his father, he had no time for political parties of the old type, so that the party he came to found contained no professional politicians. In October 1933, the Falange Española came into existence. Shortly afterwards it combined with Ledesma's J.O.N.S., on 11 February 1934, taking over its yoke and arrows symbol, but keeping control of the amalgamated group with José Antonio and another Falangist, Julio Ruiz de Alda, acting as leaders with Ledesma. The combined party held its first meeting at Valladolid on 14 March 1934, it being at once obvious that the real leader was José Antonio, now a deputy in the Cortes. He made a stirring speech at the gathering, his vigorous style being much to the taste of the audience, largely composed of disillusioned middle class men and the restless younger members of wealthier families. There was also a sprinkling of retired officers and former supporters of José

32   The Falangist leader José Antonio Primo de Rivera

33   José Calvo Sotelo

Antonio's father. It was not long before this predominantly militant group began to urge more violent action on the pacific José Antonio, who found that his followers took too literally some of his more picturesque oratory, so that by the spring of 1936 many Falangists were conducting a private civil war against their hated enemies of the Left.

With the relaxation of control now that the government was of the Centre, the Carlists suddenly become active too. All over Navarra, they could be found preparing for possible trouble. To increase their military efficiency they had persuaded Colonel Enrique Varela to come and supervise their training. He was an outstanding officer who had won a great reputation for bravery in Morocco, and, disguised as a priest with the name of Tío Pepe (Uncle Joe), he began the task of building up a Carlist army. Then on 31 March 1934, Mussolini received a small deputation led by the veteran Monarchist Antonio Goicoechea and was told of the Carlists' preparations. He at once gave them 1½ million pesetas in cash and the promise of arms. Encouraged by all this, the Carlists began to recruit and plan on a much larger scale. Should the political pendulum swing to the Left again and a rebellion break out, the Requetés, as their men were called, would be a formidable fighting group.

Under the surface, dangerous forces were now coming into existence, for the Falangists and the extreme Left were also training their younger members. The situation was thus clearly deteriorating, but when Lerroux fell, his successor, Ricardo Samper, avoided any firm political action in the hope that masterly inactivity on his

34 Nationalist postcard with Falangists and the flag of the Movement

35 Requeté (Carlist) postcard showing three generations of the Errandorena family wearing the Carlist *boina* (beret)

part might improve matters all round. The only exciting moments in the Cortes tended to occur when the former Finance Minister of Primo de Rivera was speaking. He was the Monarchist José Calvo Sotelo, who had left Spain in 1931 to return under the Amnesty Law. His attacks on the government's finance policy and its weak administration soon brought him to the forefront of the Right Wing and earned him the implacable hatred of the Left.

Two crises then faced the Samper government. The first was when the Catalan government passed a Ley de Cultivos, or agrarian law, setting up an arbitration system for settling disputes between cultivators holding land on long lease from proprietors.

36 Rioters dispersing under fire in the Puerta del Sol in
Madrid in October 1934

The central government refused to acknowledge that the Catalans had any right to act
thus, but as the Cortes went into its summer recess, the action of President Companys in
ratifying the law went unanswered. The second crisis involved the Basques, who had the
right to arrange their own taxation. They considered some of Samper's legislation
infringed this right, and held an election of municipal councillors which was also a
referendum on the matter. Many of the new mayors were arrested but released on bail,
the whole affair being left pending examination by the Cortes when it reassembled
after the summer recess.

If these were not troubles enough, there was yet another crisis building up. Since
April, Gil Robles had been making it very clear to the members of the C.E.D.A. that he
was shortly expecting to be asked to form a government himself. He came out into the
open at the end of September, declaring that he and his party would withdraw their
support for Samper's government. The Cortes duly reassembled on 1 October; Gil
Robles made his statement, and Samper resigned. But once again Gil Robles was
passed over for Lerroux who was careful to include eight of his Radicals to ensure a
majority in the Cabinet of fifteen and who also sought to appease the C.E.D.A. by
appointing three of their members. The Cabinet was announced on 4 October. The
fury of the Left was beyond bounds when it was seen that their hated enemies the
Cedistas were amongst the new ministers. On 5 October a general strike almost
paralysed the whole country. Spain was very close to a revolution.

4 Revolution and Chaos

WITHIN A FEW HOURS of the start of the general strike on 5 October, two revolutions broke out, one in Catalonia, the other in Asturias. On 6 October President Companys made a stirring speech in Barcelona in which he declared that the republic had taken up arms against the Fascists as it was in serious danger. Catalonia would also do her duty. This was a clear incitement to rebellion besides being a misrepresentation of the facts. Such an act by Companys is so out of character that it has been suggested that he was forced to come out strongly against the new central government under threat of independent action by his own party, the Esquerra (the Catalan Left). But he may have been persuaded to take a strong line by one of his Counsellors, José Dencás, who had been responsible for raising a militia force, the *Escamots*, on the Fascist model. Whatever the true reason may be, in his speech Companys had proclaimed Catalonia to be the Catalan State of the Federal Spanish Republic. The new state lasted twelve hours. General Batet, the divisional commander, arrested Companys and his cabinet – all bar Dencás, who made a successful if undignified escape via a sewer. The first rebellion had collapsed at the cost of about twenty lives in street fighting between the *Escamots* and security forces.

Unhappily the October revolution in Asturias was a much more bloody affair. Apparently carrying out plans made by the Socialists and disposing of a secret arms supply, the rising began in Oviedo and the neighbouring small towns of Mieres and Sama. The revolutionaries were the local miners, well organized and well armed, and eager to defend their cherished republic. In less than ten days 30,000 miners and workers had been mobilized. The loyalist area commander, General López Ochoa, was heavily engaged near Avilés, 15 miles from the capital, but managed to defeat the rebels there and began moving slowly on the capital. Meanwhile, in Madrid, Lerroux had taken steps to meet what was in effect civil war. Generals Francisco Franco and Manuel Goded were appointed Chiefs of Staff with specific orders to control the rising. They asked for the Foreign Legion to be made available and Lerroux agreed. At once the Legion moved north with its commander, Colonel Yagüe. Oviedo and Gijón fell to them almost immediately, and by 21 October the civil war was over. Marked by atrocities on both sides, this short but bitter struggle had cost the lives of some 300 Civil Guards, Shock Troops, and soldiers, and well over 1,000 rebels. Some 30,000 people were imprisoned, including Largo Caballero, Azaña, and Prieto, and the other Socialist leaders.

The future looked forbidding. The Asturians had been crushed but another civil war might start elsewhere. One of the more ambitious generals might be on the verge of seizing power. There seemed to be no end to all the possible troubles. In fact very little happened. There was no new rising, no military dictator made his appearance. The Left Wing seemed temporarily overwhelmed by the loss of their leaders, and the Right Wing had its own difficulties in that the Falange was weakened by a quarrel between José Antonio and Ledesma, the latter being eventually ejected. The military plotters were quiescent as more officers of the Right were now getting high posts of command. Lerroux could thus continue on his way.

The Catalan Statute was duly suspended, and the rebel and Socialist leaders were sentenced to long terms of imprisonment, apart from Prieto who had escaped, Azaña who was acquitted by the Cortes, and two minor figures who were shot. Lerroux then proposed to revise the Constitution and introduce a budget. Neither got very far as one of his ministers resigned and there was a change of government with a new Prime Minister, Joaquín Chapaprieta, Lerroux becoming his Foreign Minister – though not for long. A financial scandal blew up over a gambling scheme proposed by a Dutchman, Daniel Strauss, the scheme depending on a new type of roulette wheel known as a *straperlo*. Lerroux's nephew was implicated and Lerroux himself came under suspicion of complicity in the racket and resigned. Chapaprieta then fell out with the C.E.D.A. so Gil Robles and his allies also resigned. The republic faced its twenty-sixth government crisis on 31 December 1935.

On 1 January 1936 President Alcalá Zamora suspended the Cortes for a month, then, a week later, changed his mind and dissolved it. Elections were to be held on 16 February. A temporary government was installed under Manuel Portela and the censorship was lifted. In the pre-election period, Gil Robles and the C.E.D.A. tried to gain support by an intensive poster campaign, but as they were dubious about the outcome, they took the precaution of forming alliances with Monarchists, Carlists, Agrarians, and Independents – the combined parties being given the name of the National Front. There was a mixed group of candidates in the Centre, Lerroux and the Radicals, Alcalá Zamora's Progressives, the Catalan Lliga and the Basques, and Portela's new Centre Party. On the Left, the Communists had suggested forming a Popular Front, which was set up with the Socialists and Trotskyists, but not the Anarchists, who remained on their own. The Popular Front programme was a vigorous one. The victims of the 1934 revolution were to be reinstated and indemnified. The

37   President Companys and members of the Catalan
Government

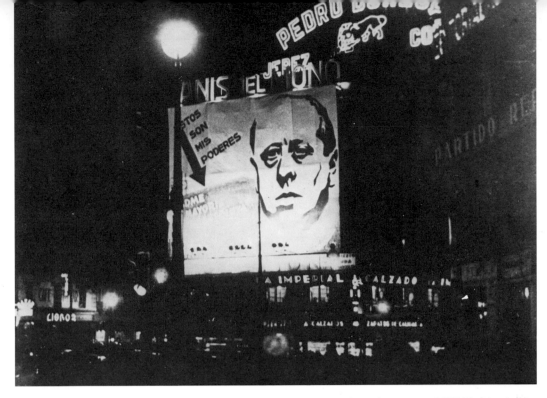

38   1936 Elections. A gigantic poster of Gil Robles in the
Puerta del Sol, Madrid

Catalan Statute of Autonomy would be restored, and various reforms put in hand at
once. After saying what they planned to do to save Spain, both sides spent the rest of
the time vilifying each other. Terms like 'Vatican Fascists' or 'Marxist Revolutionaries' were comparatively mild examples. But in spite of all this wordy violence, the
actual elections passed off calmly, the final results being:

Left Wing (Popular Front)   278 (+179)
Right Wing (National Front) 134 (− 73)
Centre   55 (−112)

The elections of February 1936 show the strength of the swing back to the Left,
particularly at the expense of the Centre which was now very much an unstable
collection of small groups, the biggest being Portela's Centre Party, the Lliga, and the
Basques. Only four seats were finally held for Lerroux's Radicals. On the Right, the
C.E.D.A. was by far the largest party, having eighty-eight seats, with the Monarchists,
now led by Calvo Sotelo, holding thirteen. On the Left, the Socialists were the main
group with ninety-nine seats, whilst the Republican Left held eighty-seven. This latter
total is of interest as this party was led by Azaña. After suffering a steep decline in his
political reputation over matters like the Catalan revolution in which he was implicated,
Azaña began to recover his position steadily to become one of the really powerful men
of the Left during the Civil War. The interpretation of the election figures has given rise
to much argument, as some deputies moved from one group to another. The overall
votes cast can be made to show an almost equal division in the country as a whole. If
one includes the Basques with the Left Wing, that group obtained 4,306,156 votes

39 Cartoon showing the ministers of the first Republican Government

against 4,464,648 for the Right. If the Basques are counted with the Right, the figures become 4,176,156 against 4,594,648. But from the point of reality, the Popular Front won 278 seats and were back in control. What was even worse for the men of the Centre and Right, Azaña was the new Prime Minister and there were a lot of old scores to be paid off.

An interesting sidelight on subsequent events is afforded by an interview which General Franco had with the caretaker Prime Minister, Portela, a day or two after the elections. The Chief of Staff suggested that the declaration of a State of War by Portela would block the Popular Front's assumption of power. When the Prime Minister said this would inevitably lead to a revolution, Franco's reply was that there was enough force available to crush any revolt. Shortly afterwards, Calvo Sotelo urged the same course of action on behalf of the Monarchists he now led. But Portela took no heed and handed over to Azaña in the normal way. Generals Orgaz and Ponte of the original plotters then met Generals Franco, Fanjul, Mola (the Moroccan Commander), and Varela. The sensible decision was taken to wait before taking any definite action.

The Azaña Cabinet set to work at once to revive the former Republican ideals by pushing forward the agrarian reforms much more quickly, and compensating those who had suffered from the events of October 1934 from the pockets of the employers who had dismissed them. General Franco was posted to the Canary Islands, whilst General Goded was hurried off to a like post in the Balearics. The heroes of October 1934 had become more or less the exiles of March 1936. General Emilio Mola was switched from Morocco to Pamplona as a precaution. Before leaving for their new positions the three met a number of other officers, amongst them Generals Fanjul, Orgaz, Ponte, and Varela. The majority decision was to support any military revolt if widespread collapse threatened or if Largo Caballero was offered the Premiership. The preparations for such a contingency now went ahead with Mola as the real brain behind the organization.

The immediate aftermath of the electoral victory was a nationwide and almost exuberant outburst of violence due largely to the excitement of the newly released prisoners, but with more sinister undertones. In vain José Antonio Primo de Rivera had tried to restrain any violent action by his Falangists. Many of them believed that if the present disorders were increased by further shooting and provocation, a situation would soon arise which would sweep the Right back into power. The Falange, aided by paid gunmen (*pistoleros*), fought a private running battle with the Socialist extremists, particularly the followers of Largo Caballero who had spent much of the time during his recent stay in prison reading the works of Marx and Engels, and who had become more and more revolutionary in his speeches, having finally split with the more moderate Prieto. By about April 1936, the Left was tending to fall apart, whilst the Right was firmly closing its ranks, with Calvo Sotelo now the leading Opposition spokesman in the Cortes.

Azaña's reaction to the growing panic was to turn on the Falange, its Madrid

40   Madrid 1936. A Popular Front demonstration

headquarters being abruptly closed on 27 February. In an attempt to control its more violent members, José Antonio was imprisoned as a hostage for their behaviour. These moves failed and the shootings continued. Then further trouble flared up, this time on the Left when the peasants began taking over the sequestrated lands in the south on their own initiative. They were left unmolested.

It now seemed obvious that the real moment of crisis was fast approaching. General Mola, once Director-General of Security in 1931, was almost an ideal planner for the new revived conspiracy. He drafted and distributed his master plan early in April. There was to be one civil and one military plot with sections organized all over Spain, the Balearics, the Canary Islands, and Morocco. Each section was to prepare plans to take over all public buildings and seize communications. Very little was said of the Falange which was only mentioned in regard to the projected rising in Seville. The signal for the rising would be given at the end of April. With his characteristic attention to detail, Mola was clearly taking no risks.

The next political sensation was the removal of Alcalá Zamora from the Presidency. He had made enemies amongst both the Left and the Right by his legalistic attitude to affairs, and when Indalecio Prieto asked for his deposition on 7 April, his days were literally numbered. A censure motion was introduced into the Cortes under the article of the Constitution permitting such a move after the President had dissolved Cortes twice. It was duly passed and Alcalá Zamora's term came to a sudden end. He took a

41   Madrid 1936, street arrests. The suspect is handcuffed to a detective

42   General Emilio Mola

43 President Azaña (*right*) with the Speaker of the Cortes,
Martínez Barrio

rest from the cares of state by going on a long holiday abroad, thus missing the start of the rising which was to destroy the republic completely.

His departure made no difference in fact as the assassinations and shootings only grew. There was a pitched battle in Madrid on 17 April when Falangists and Socialist Youth members fought each other in the East Cemetery during the funeral of a Civil Guard officer. It was at this point that the Falange began winning new members by the thousand. With the approach of the deadline for the military rising, disaster seemed very close at hand. But the expected signal was not given. On 18 April, General Rodríguez Barrio, who was to set the plan in motion in Madrid, had second thoughts, and Varela had to telephone round countermanding the orders already given. The delay meant that General Sanjurjo, who was still in Portugal and trying to persuade a Carlist group to join the plot, had time to press his arguments.

On 1 May the Labour Day celebrations were on a vast scale with large numbers of Socialist and Communist Youth members on parade in uniform like troops. From his prison José Antonio now issued a directive to the Falange urging co-operation with the military should the army take action.

Then, on 10 May, the presidential election took place, and by 238 votes to 5, Manuel Azaña was elected. How far he himself engineered this, it is difficult to say. He may have felt that he would have more effective power as President to control events. At any rate, he moved over to the Presidential Palace and Santiago Casares Quiroga became the next Prime Minister.

Mola now began to reorganize his plot. On 25 May he sent out details of a new plan. Two days later a letter was sent to him by José Antonio promising Falangist help. On 3 June the first discussions with the Carlists began in Pamplona. Mola then issued a further directive on the organization to be set up after the rising had begun. On the model of Primo de Rivera's government, there was to be a governing council of officers consisting of a President and four members, to be known as the Directory. An

44 Madrid 1936. A riot in progress near the Spanish Parliament building

assembly would be elected to act as a ratifying body. But if he had hoped to secure Carlist support for this scheme he was to be disappointed because Fal Conde, the Carlist leader, turned it down on 10 June. Mola tried to persuade him to accept, but he still refused, adding a further objection, namely, that the plan for the rising included a statement that it was to be conducted under the Monarchist flag. Only when Sanjurjo intervened by letter from Portugal were the two men reconciled. But all this negotiation had meant that Mola was forced to tell his fellow conspirators on 1 July that they would have to be patient for a while longer. At least he now knew that if all went well his planning would soon show results, so the next step in the plot was taken.

When the rising started, General Franco was to be conveyed from the Canary Islands to Morocco to assume command of the army there. So Luis Bolín of *A.B.C.* arranged with a charter company in London to fly a plane to Las Palmas. The pilot was Captain Bebb, and a party consisting of Major Hugh Pollard, his daughter, and one of her friends left on 11 July. The expedition was a normal holiday trip, and only Bolín, who went with them as far as Casablanca, knew what the real purpose was.

Then on 12 July an officer of the Shock Troops, one Lieutenant José Castillo, was shot dead by gunmen. A Captain Condés of the Civil Guard suggested that as a reprisal Calvo Sotelo and Gil Robles should be arrested. Gil Robles was on holiday in Biarritz and so escaped. But Calvo Sotelo was at home when Condés arrived on the night of 12–13 July. He made no objection to the arrest and was driven away. Next day his corpse was identified in the morgue of Madrid's East Cemetery.

The generals' conspiracy now had a martyr, but there are no grounds for the suggestion made at the time that the murder was the factor which led to the actual rising four days later. Mola was a meticulous planner, not an improviser. It is far more likely that the date was determined by another event – the final agreement by the Carlists to the proposed arrangements. The death of Calvo Sotelo seems to have been the immediate reason for Prince François Xavier of Bourbon-Parma and Fal Conde declaring their support in a document signed by them at St Jean de Luz. Mola now issued an instruction containing the information that the rising would start at 1700 hours on 17 July, and would begin in Morocco. General Goded would proceed from the Balearics to Barcelona to lead the revolt there, General Franco would come to Morocco to direct the campaign there and in the south, whilst Mola himself would control the north, all three eventually converging on Madrid. General Sanjurjo would fly in from his exile in Portugal. Mola also sent details through to José Antonio who had been transferred from Madrid to Alicante for greater security.

The government spent the day on 13 July in trying to keep control of events. The Madrid offices of potential trouble-makers were closed down, Anarchists, Monarchists, and Carlists all being treated alike. Casares Quiroga refused to allow arms to be handed to the workers from government stocks, but numbers of militiamen had already been armed from their party supplies of weapons. On 14 July Lieutenant Castillo's funeral took place in the East Cemetery – a few hours afterwards Calvo Sotelo was also buried there. Tension rose alarmingly all day, and that night the militia maintained their watch on their enemies. On 15 July the Permanent Committee of the Cortes met to hear first a formal speech by the Conde de Vallellano protesting at the killing of Calvo Sotelo, then an attack by Gil Robles on the government's incompetence. He then

45   Cartoon of Casares Quiroga, Prime Minister at the outbreak of the Civil War, from *El Sol*, May 1936

The Dilemma of Casares Quiroga:
Bullfighter: Either you settle our grievance or we go on strike.
Minister (Casares Quiroga): No hombre, no. The other way round. You get the grievance settled for me or you go out on strike, whether you want to or not.

43

took the wise precaution of leaving to continue his interrupted holiday in Biarritz – one narrow escape was enough.

The day before that appointed for the revolt saw the arrest of some Falangists and a certain hardening of the government's attitude towards the Right. General Varela was arrested in Cadiz where he was putting the last touches to his plans. General Franco was still in Tenerife but had been told his plane was now at Las Palmas on Gran Canaria. Fate stepped in at this point to help him on his way, as the Military Governor of Las Palmas, General Amadeo Balmes, contrived to kill himself when doing some shooting practice, and Franco had a very good reason to ask (and obtain) permission to go to Las Palmas – to attend the funeral. On the mainland the last-minute instructions were being issued. At last all was ready.

46   Civil Guards searching Madrid demonstrators for arms

5 'Nothing to Report'

THE RISING was timed to start at 1700 hours on 18 July after the leading garrison commanders and others involved had received by telegram the ironic codeword 'Sin novedad' – 'Nothing to report'. If all went according to plan, it seemed very possible that the Republican supporters would be overwhelmed by the strength of the forces against them and would only offer token resistance. In fact, the civil war lasted for just over two and a half years. Amongst other reasons, the violence of Left Wing reaction and the powers of improvization of the Republicans seem to have been seriously underestimated, and no one foresaw the possibility of foreign intervention or its effects. In addition, both sides at times found that otherwise sound courses of action were suddenly jeopardized by quite unforeseeable accidents.

One such accident, which occurred before the deadline, could have had serious consequences for the rebels in that it led to the Moroccan rising starting a day earlier than planned. If the Republican government had judged the position correctly and had reacted vigorously, General Mola and his associates in Spain would have met with much stiffer resistance in the crucial early days of the war.

On the morning of 17 July Colonel Seguí told the officers of the Melilla garrison of the plans for revolt. This information was also passed to the local Falangists, and was betrayed by one of them to the pro-Republican Commander, General Romerales. When the conspirators returned to the headquarters map room after lunch, a Lieutenant Zaro arrived with some troops and orders to conduct a search. When these orders had been confirmed by the general on the telephone, Colonel Gazapo rang a unit of the Foreign Legion and ordered them to come to his relief. The Lieutenant hesitated and then surrendered. Colonel Seguí went at once to Romerales and forced him to resign at pistol point.

The officers then occupied all the public buildings in Melilla, and after a short skirmish with groups of workers and party officials, the wholesale arrest of all Republican supporters was carried out, and the town was firmly in rebel hands. When the news reached Madrid, General Gómez Morato was contacted in Larache and flew to Melilla to deal with the situation, only to be arrested when he landed.

Later in the afternoon of 17 July, Colonel Sáenz de Buruaga, who was to lead the Tetuán rising, was informed of the events at Melilla. With Colonels Asensio and Beigbeder he went into action, besieging the High Commissioner, Álvarez Buylla, in his residence and stamping out all opposition except at the airfield, where Major Puente held out till the next day. On 19 July General Franco landed there from Las Palmas.

At Ceuta, Colonel Yagüe was completely in control by 2300 hours, but there was severe fighting at Larache where the rising began at 0200 hours on the 18th. Some officers and the trade unions remained loyal and managed to maintain their resistance until dawn. All opponents were then arrested and some shot. Elsewhere there was little opposition so that by the morning of the 18th all Spanish Morocco was in rebel hands.

Before leaving for Morocco General Franco had taken over Las Palmas with the aid of General Orgaz and had issued his first manifesto. This was a statement in general terms on the lines that the army felt itself to be the protector of Spain's true interests

47 General Queipo de Llano, 'the Radio General'

48 [*opposite*] Granada Front Militiamen advancing to attack an enemy position

and would bring a new and better life to all Spaniards. There was no reference to the church's position in the struggle or in the promised new régime. At this point and for some time afterwards the leaders of the rising saw themselves as leaders of a military crusade and their object as the restoration of Spain in terms of the military virtues of duty and discipline.

Almost at the moment this manifesto was being broadcast throughout Morocco, the first essential stage of the rising had been completed. Colonel Yagüe had sent off the 'Sin novedad' telegrams to the garrisons in Spain in the evening of 17 July; twelve hours later he must have felt much more confident of success. General Franco and his officers now had at their disposal the 32,000 trained officers and men of the Foreign Legion. If these could be transported to Spain, there was every hope that resistance would quickly collapse. But there still remained the problem of how to get them across to Spain, and the solution depended on the progress of the rising there and on the position in the navy.

The news of the Melilla rebellion led Prime Minister Casares Quiroga and his government to adopt two courses of immediate action. The first was to encourage all high officials in Morocco to organize resistance, the second was to order naval vessels to Morocco from the bases of Cartagena and El Ferrol. The apparent view that this was a local affair seems to be confirmed by a statement broadcast early on 18 July by Radio Madrid that the plot would be firmly dealt with, and that it had no support in Spain itself. But shortly after this denial the first risings in Andalusia were reported, and Casares Quiroga faced a classic dilemma. He had firmly rejected all pleas for arms to be distributed to Left Wing organizations and had ordered all Civil Governors not to give out any weapons. By so doing and by keeping to constitutional methods, his government practically ensured the success of the second stage of the rising and the setting-up of a firm bridgehead in the south for the reception of troops from Morocco. In their desire to avoid the problem of how to control armed irregulars, the more

46

moderate Republicans in power were to find themselves faced with a worse problem – how to control a revolution started by their more ardent supporters alarmed at the deteriorating situation in Andalusia.

There a valuable bridgehead had been secured at once on 18 July with the successful capture of La Línea, Algeciras, Jérez de la Frontera, and Cadiz. There was some fierce, sporadic resistance which was subdued when the first small contingent of Moroccan troops arrived on the next day. This was followed by the capture of Seville by a remarkable combination of bluff and opportunism on the part of General Queipo de Llano, Commander of the Carabineros.

This officer arrived in the city on 17 July with only four other officers to support him. He began his campaign on the morning of the 18th by arresting the Garrison Commander, General Villa Abrile, with his staff. At the infantry barracks he then found the Colonel in charge was a loyal Republican so he calmly deprived him of his command, locked him up with his officers, and replaced him with a captain. He next went to the artillery barracks to find that there the officers came over to his side without demur. Under the threat of their guns the Civil Governor surrendered, with the result that the Civil Guard now joined him. Whilst the workers were hurriedly organizing resistance, he took over the radio station and began his famous series of broadcast commentaries. Next day the suburbs were still fiercely held by Republicans, but reinforcements flown in from Morocco attacked the Triana area on 20 July and quickly reduced the rest of the city. The main obstacle to any expansion northwards had fallen in two days.

Córdoba was taken over by Colonel Cascajo, the Military Governor, with hardly any opposition, but at Granada General Campins remained loyal with the support of the Popular Front. Finally, on 20 July, Colonels Muñoz and León succeeded in starting a revolt and in capturing Campins. With the aid of artillery and infantry officers, the Civil Guard and the Assault Guards, they occupied the major part of the

49 General Varela

city with the exception of El Albaicín which was not taken until 24 July after heavy losses had been inflicted on the suburb's defenders.

The immediate need was to clear the country between these isolated strongpoints to form one solid block of territory. Apart from Granada, this was accomplished in a few days with a Civil Guard rising in Huelva and the use of fast moving groups of soldiers from Africa. Contact was finally made with Granada by a Moroccan force under General Varela, who was forced to halt further advance eastwards to deal with a dangerous threat to Córdoba, where the Republican General Miaja and the local militia had reached the city area on 20 August, only to be put to flight by the sudden arrival of Varela's small but well-trained force.

In the meantime, the disasters of those first two days of the campaign had had profound repercussions outside Andalusia. Casares Quiroga resigned late in the night of 18 July, and President Azaña appointed Martínez Barrio to replace him with instructions to attempt to negotiate with the rebels. But both General Mola in Pamplona and General Cabanellas in Saragossa rejected any such step. So very early on 19 July Azaña made a further effort to solve the problem by asking José Giral to become Prime Minister. He took over with the support of the Socialists, Communists, and Anarchists, and at once issued an order that all arms available were to be issued to the Trade Unions everywhere. His action undoubtedly saved the day in a number of towns, but in others the order was received too late to have any effect on the course of events. On 19 July the rebels made significant gains in the more traditionalist and conservative provinces.

General Mola had no problem with Navarra which was solidly Carlist, nor did Aragón offer any real resistance. In Castile the old capital of Burgos came over at once, whilst in Valladolid violent fighting developed round the main railway station area and lasted all day. Towns like Segovia and Ávila declared their support at once, whilst León waited until a trainload of Asturian miners were safely on their way back north before rising successfully on 20 July. Further south the town and the province of Cáceres joined the movement. By 20 July a wide strip of rebel-held territory separated the Government provinces in Asturias and the Basque Country from the main Republican zone, and there was every chance that this strip would shortly be linked up to the southern bridgehead along the Portuguese border.

The isolated northern Republican area consisted of the Basque provinces of Guipúzcoa and Vizcaya, Álava having been occupied, the province of Santander, Asturias, and northern Galicia. By 24 July this last western end of the zone had fallen to the rebels. In Corunna the town was still under the control of the Popular Front until the 21st, but at about 1300 hours the organizer of the rising, Colonel Martín Alonso, suddenly arrested the area Commander and the Military Governor and his forces took the centre of the port. Forty-eight hours later he had succeeded in clearing the whole area. At the naval base of El Ferrol on the other side of the bay, the ratings on the *Almirante Cervera* and the *España* fought off the rebels for most of the 21st, but eventually surrendered, so that the latter's naval strength had gained a base and ships.

The only other rebel success in the region was at Oviedo, where the Garrison Commander, Colonel Aranda, waited until some 4,000 of the fiercely Republican miners near there had been misled by the apparent lack of activity to travel to more vital areas where danger might threaten. With the local Civil and Assault Guards and the Falangists he had no difficulty in taking the city, but next day was himself besieged in it.

50 Asturian Front 1937. A captured Republican 'armoured' car on show in Oviedo

At the end of the first three days of fighting the overall picture must have been an alarming one for the Madrid Government. Approximately half the total area of Spain and Spanish Morocco had been lost to them, and worse was clearly going to befall very soon if General Franco succeeded in transporting his Moroccan troops to Spain. Time was needed to co-ordinate armed resistance but if they moved still loyal troops from the towns now held, there was always the possibility of further risings occurring. On the credit side, although Majorca and Ibiza had fallen, the attempted risings in Valencia, Alicante, and Almería had been contained or crushed and only Albacete had been lost. Also, on 20 July, General Sanjurjo, on his way to join his comrades from his exile in Portugal, had been killed in an air crash. If the industrial regions of Spain could be firmly held and further rebel advances slowed or checked, there could possibly be a swing of events in the government's favour. But three major urgent problems had to be tackled now. The first was due to the political tensions which had resulted from the violent popular reaction to the rebellion, the second and third concerned the situation developing in Madrid and Barcelona, where recent events had produced a revolutionary movement aimed at forcing the government into effective action.

The sequence of events began in Barcelona before dawn on 19 July when troops from the barracks round the city began to move towards the central Plaza de Cataluña. The plan to take over the city from the centre outwards was not unsound in theory, but the planners had over-simplified the situation. They had failed to ensure the security of some of the local depots of arms, so thay were unaware that weapons had been distributed to the Anarchist workers. They also failed to take into account the hostility of the Civil Guard towards the military. Almost at once, the rebel troops were halted by thousands of workers, supported by groups of well-trained Civil and Assault Guards. Only one column reached the Plaza, to be decimated there; other troops turned on their officers. General Goded, who had flown from Majorca to take command, was penned in the Captaincy General alongside the port where he was taken prisoner. In the face of the disaster which had overtaken his men, he agreed to broadcast an appeal to them to stop fighting. Apart from one or two points of resistance which were soon stormed, the battle was over and Barcelona was firmly in the control of an Anarchist revolutionary group.

The rising in Madrid also began on 19 July and was centred in the various barracks

51   Troops barricaded in the Barcelona Telephone Exchange

52   Desecration of the Jesuit Church at
Vallecas near Madrid during 1936

53   Republican soldiers and machine-
gun post in Madrid

round the city, the fiercest and bloodiest fighting taking place at the Montaña Barracks
on the west side, held by General Fanjul, the leader of the revolt in the capital. As in
Barcelona, the workers had received a quantity of weapons, but here the rebels seem to
have had no prearranged plan of action, and the size of the crowds made any sortie
impossible. On 20 July, after a fairly heavy shelling, the Montaña Barracks was stormed
and most of the rebel defenders massacred. Shortly afterwards the Carabanchel
barracks fell, and very soon all the others were captured or had surrendered. The
officers in the northern barracks of El Pardo escaped to the rebel lines.

The political outcome of the struggle in Madrid was that President Azaña and the
government were still nominally in control, but the real power lay with the Socialists
and particularly with the Unión General de Trabajadores (U.G.T.). On the military
side there were now some 10,000 militiamen eager to annihilate the rebels, even if they
were only armed as far as the supply of weapons went. Much the same had happened
in Barcelona, where President Companys was still in office but with Anarchists really
the dominant force, and where an army was being hurriedly formed to march against
General Mola in Navarra and Aragón. It was also quite obvious as a result of the
fierceness of the fighting that all possibility of negotiation or compromise had utterly
vanished, and that the initial rebellion was rapidly turning into a large-scale war, so
that the next step both in Barcelona and Madrid was necessarily that of creating
properly led armies out of the unorganized groups of loyal troops and raw militiamen.

The consequent sharpening of the conflict was accompanied by increased violence
on both sides in the attempt to destroy all potential traitors to the cause. The rebel areas
came increasingly under martial law and summary executions of actual or suspected
pro-Republicans were widespread. On the Republican side there was a similar situation with much destruction of church property and many executions of churchmen,

as well as of rebel sympathizers or supporters. Civil wars almost invariably bring with them such destruction of life and property, much of it arising from a need to frighten others into submission, or from a fear that an enemy left alive is a potential danger, or from a desire to obtain revenge for past injury, real or imagined.

The number of those who died in this way is very difficult to determine as no records were kept, and individuals only too frequently took advantage of the confusion to shoot down their personal or political enemies. However, some idea of the extent of the killings can be gained by an analysis of population figures where available, and a critical examination of quoted statistics, provided some allowance is made for some deaths actually occurring in military action and no figure is accepted without some supporting evidence. The total supplied by the Nationalists after the war ended and inscribed on the Sanctuary at Valladolid was 54,594 civilians, to which must be added some 6,832 religious persons of all kinds. This gives a combined total of 61,426 Nationalists killed. It is much harder to establish a figure for Republican deaths because of the difficulty of establishing the cause of death, but a realistic approximation would seem to lie between 50,000 and 70,000. The dead included military personnel, churchmen, monks, nuns, intellectuals, professors, teachers, deputies, mayors, nobility, middle class citizens, workers, farmers, peasants, old and young. The symbol of this tragic destruction of life is the **Andalusian** poet, **Federico García Lorca**, shot on 18 August 1936.

54   Column of Republican troops on the march

55   Nationalist column moving forward to new positions

6 On to Madrid

THE NEXT STAGE to consider is the so-called 'Battle of the Sierras', the struggle for control of the chain north of Madrid comprising the Sierra de Gredos and the Sierra de Guadarrama. This complex and wide system of mountains and twisting valleys often with steep sides is a formidable barrier from which the plains to the north and south can be controlled. As the terrain is so difficult, control of the few roads crossing the area forms the key to the pattern the battle assumed. The two main roads from the north were the main axes of advance and fierce fighting quickly developed round the Somosierra Pass on the Burgos–Madrid road, and the Alto del León on the Valladolid highway. Both these passes had been seized by militia forces rushed up from Madrid, but a column sent to take Ávila, under Colonel Mangada, halted at Navalperal apparently because its commander did not fancy being at the end of a long and tenuous line of communication. When the column withdrew a serious potential threat to the rebel build-up was removed. Similar lapses of co-ordination by Republican army commanders show how the lack of a really firm central military high command could turn possible victory into probable defeat.

The rebels' reaction was to throw in every available man from the Ávila and Segovia areas to block the enemy's path so that time could be gained for bringing up regular forces from further back. The counter-attack began on 19 July with an attempt to outflank the eastern end of the mountain chain by a thrust aimed at Guadalajara via Logroño, Soria, and Sigüenza. This was entrusted by General Mola to Colonel García Escámez at the head of about 1,000 regulars, Carlists and Falangists. But the column delayed at Logroño to ensure that the rather half-hearted support for the rising shown there was no real danger; the Madrid militia thus won the race to Guadalajara. The rebel force was too small to clear them out so this key town covering the valley leading to Alcalá and Madrid was not secured. The column retraced its steps to the north of Sigüenza, swung west to Aranda de Duero, then turned south to reinforce the small group of rebels who had seized the Somosierra tunnel. It arrived at an opportune moment because militia from Guadalajara were moving north to the same area. These troops fought with great ferocity, but blind courage not supported by adequate training and firepower was no match for regular soldiers, whose experience was combined with superior artillery. The Somosierra Pass was completely in rebel hands by 25 July.

A similar situation arose at the Alto del León where the rebel attack had begun when a column under Colonel Serrador arrived from Valladolid on 22 July. The actual battle followed the Somosierra pattern but was shorter as the pass was under rebel control by the end of the same day. The result of the Sierra fighting was high losses for the Republicans, who, though they still held the crests of the mountains between, were now split by two small salients thrusting southwards down two of the main routes to Madrid from the north. On the other hand, they held Guadalajara, blocking any further thrust from the north-east.

Elsewhere in the north-east the military situation was slightly to the advantage of the republic as Barcelona had reacted vigorously to a report that the rebels were about

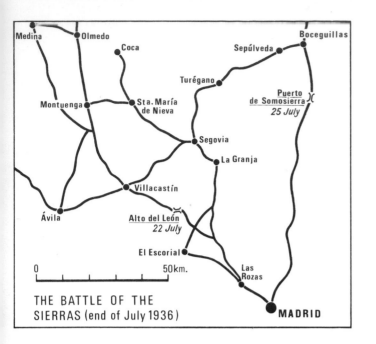

THE BATTLE OF THE
SIERRAS (end of July 1936)

MAP 2
THE BATTLE OF THE SIERRAS.
(i) The Alto del León was defended
by Colonel Castillo and stormed
by Colonel Serrador (22 July); (ii)
The Somosierra Pass was attacked
by Captain Calán and cleared by
Colonel García Escámez (25 July)

to advance on Catalonia from Saragossa. The report was in fact false, but a column of about 1,000 Anarchists and a few regulars set out to take Saragossa under the leadership of the anarchist leader Durruti with Colonel Pérez Farrás as military director. The move began on 23 July, and was joined by other columns all moving west into the province of Huesca. Little resistance was met for a time and those few points where the rebels had gained the upper hand were quickly retaken so that by the end of a fortnight there was a rough front established running almost due north and south slightly to the east of a line Jaca–Huesca–Saragossa–Belchite–Teruel, where it curved north-westwards to the Guadalajara area. There this force of revolutionary militiamen halted to prepare a defence system of strongpoints ready for the attack on Saragossa itself. The presence of numerous foreign volunteer detachments with this force is the first stage in the formation of the International Brigades. Most of these early volunteers were Germans or Italians, but there were a few French and English and one or two other nationals, both Communists and Socialists.

Pressure had also been put on the Basque Provinces by General Mola, who had set in motion a three-pronged drive north on 22 July against San Sebastián, Leaburu, and Tolosa. One aim of this diversion was to close the frontier, an initial success in this plan being the capture of Oyarzún, very close to the road to Irún. But before this gain was to be exploited, a much more important rebel advance began in the south, resulting in the linking-up of the early bridgehead and the main area to the north. The campaign occupied the period from 6 August to 3 September when Talavera de la Reina fell and the road to Madrid from the west was clear. To achieve this success the rebel command had to solve a major problem – the transfer of the bulk of the Army of Africa to the mainland. The republic still had enough warships to make transport by sea a hazardous operation. The rebel fleet was of no great power and in the south there were only about a dozen aircraft to provide cover.

In this position it was obvious that if aircraft could be obtained, the build-up could be carried out safely and swiftly. General Franco had already sent Captain Luis

54

56　The airlift, July
1936. German Junker 52s
which transported troops
of the Army of Africa at
a vital stage of the rising

Bolín to Rome where he arrived on 21 July. The Foreign Minister, Count Ciano, was eager to help, and under further pressure from Spain, Mussolini agreed on 24 July to send aid as requested. The next step was an approach to Germany and this was made to the German Military Attaché in Paris on 22 July, ten transport planes being requested for supply to Spanish Morocco. A deputation was also sent off with a letter to Herr Hitler. On 26 July the Führer also agreed to help the rebels. In both cases, immediate assistance was given by the despatch to Morocco of a number of aircraft, twelve from the Italians and thirty from the Germans. The airlift could start at once with the aid of these latter Junkers 52 transports, whilst the former machines covered movement of troops and heavy equipment by sea. Active foreign intervention in the Civil War had begun and was to increase quickly as both sides strove to gain military superiority.

 In a few days some 4,000 reinforcements had gathered at Seville to await General Franco's arrival on 6 August. He directed the campaign, but the actual field commander was Colonel Yagüe, whose style of leadership was ideally suited to the type of operation envisaged. His normal procedure was to use small groups of lorry-borne infantry which were pushed forward as fast as possible with their accompanying artillery. Any resistance was heavily shelled, then a vigorous attack was mounted to break up any remaining pockets. In five days he covered the 300 kilometres from Seville to Mérida, his only set battle being at the river Guadiana just south of the latter town. He then swung west to take Badajoz whilst another column beat off a violent Republican attack by local militia and troops thrown in from Madrid. Badajoz was stormed on 14 August and taken amid scenes of ferocious carnage. A week later Yagüe was on the move again, this time leading a two-pronged drive to the Madrid–Plasencia road. One column followed the route via Trujillo to Navalmoral de la Mata, whilst a second force drove through the west end of the Sierra de Guadalupe making for the same objective. The Republican Army of Extremadura was covering the Tagus crossing, and the second rebel column came under aerial bombardment by a French volunteer

55

squadron, but it escaped serious loss. The vastly superior training of this column's troops forced the Republicans to withdraw and the link-up was made. The advance was renewed almost at once, the Republican forces falling back steadily to Talavera de la Reina where a stand was made covering the town. Yagüe opened his attack on 3 September though outnumbered three to one. Such was the violence of his main assault that resistance collapsed and by late afternoon Talavera was in his hands. By this brilliant if risky operation he had linked up with the northern rebel zone and had driven to within 115 kilometres of Madrid.

At this point, General Franco found himself in a dilemma. He had received a further 10,000 men from Morocco and Yagüe was in an ideal position to make for the Spanish capital. But what could have been a straightforward decision was complicated by one factor. In the old city of Toledo a rebel garrison was grimly holding out in the Alcázar against all Republican attempts to annihilate it. Since 20 July Colonel Moscardó of the Toledo Military Academy had been defending his fortress tenaciously at the head of about 1,100 army officers, Civil Guards, and Falangists, and some 200 cadets whom he had rounded up in Madrid. He had also brought into the Alcázar about 600 women and children, and had not forgotten to include the Republican Civil Governor and about 100 hostages. The Alcázar swimming-bath provided a water supply though food was scarce. The nearby arms factory ensured an adequate supply of ammunition, and morale was high. But there was a complete lack of any information as to what was happening outside Toledo, so that the garrison's reactions can easily be imagined when a plane flew over them on 17 August, dropping messages from General Franco and General Mola, and giving them their first news of the initial success of the rising.

Colonel Yagüe began moving forward again after regrouping, reaching Maqueda on 21 September. In the meantime the Alcázar had survived the destruction of its

57   Siege of the Alcázar. General
Moscardó taken just after the relief   58   Column of Spanish Moroccan troops

MAP 3

SEVILLE TO TOLEDO. An Army
of Africa force under Colonel
Yagüe was divided into three
groups each of 825 men plus
artillery. It reached Talavera on 3
September and Maqueda on 21
September. It was then diverted
under General Varela to Toledo
which was relieved on 27
September.

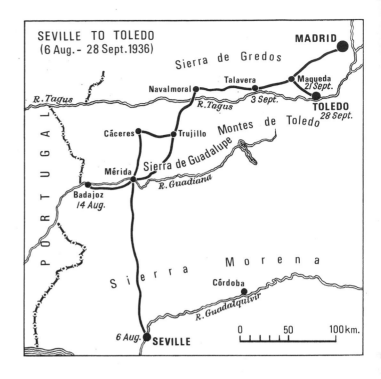

south-east tower on 18 September, and an attempt to set it on fire on the 20th. The
Prime Minister, Largo Caballero, came down from Madrid to supervise the final
assault and mining was begun under the north-east tower. Then, on 21 September,
General Franco ordered his troops to go to the relief of the beleaguered garrison, and
as Yagüe had been taken ill, General Varela himself took charge. Before he could
reach Toledo, the new mine was exploded on 25 September, the government promptly
issuing a communiqué claiming the capture of the fortress – in an excess of optimism as
Moscardó's men were still holding on. Their stubbornness was rewarded on 27 September when they could see to the north the dark lines of troops of the relieving army
moving into position. That evening the Moroccans got through, and the next day
Moscardó greeted Varela with the laconic phrase 'sin novedad'. Franco may have lost
the chance to take Madrid, but at least he had the arms factory as compensation.

By the end of September, the military situation round Madrid was deteriorating
rapidly from the Republican point of view. The line in the Sierras north of the capital
still held, whilst Guadalajara protected Madrid from attack from the east, but with
the relief of Toledo accomplished, the growing forces to the west and south-west were
clearly not going to stay where they were. Already in the previous month the madrileños had had a foretaste of what was to come. Raids by small groups of bombers
occurred on 23 August (Getafe aerodrome), 25 August (Cuatro Vientos aerodrome),
27–28–29 August (Madrid). The government began devising a system of air raid
precautions with warnings by siren and the enforcement of a blackout.

As yet the republic had received little aid from abroad to counterbalance the
supplies from Italy and Germany now reaching the rebels in a steady flow. An approach
had been made to France at the end of July, and after much hesitation Léon Blum, the
Prime Minister, had been forced to make a public rejection of the request for aid, but

59   A German 88-millimetre
anti-aircraft gun of the Condor Legion.
German experts trained Nationalists
how to use the most modern equipment

60   Málaga Campaign. Nationalist
troops in a landing

had agreed that a shipment would be made by routing it via Mexico. The novelist André Malraux made himself the unofficial intermediary, acting as buyer for the Republican purchasing commission set up in the Paris Spanish Embassy. Aid from Communist sources outside Spain was also sought, but as Stalin was very concerned to preserve his alliance with France, the first supplies only covered food and similar items together with money. Some of the funds needed were collected through various organizations of an outwardly humanitarian type asking for help for the Spanish people and mostly run by committees of outstanding public figures, although the administration was nearly always carried out by a Communist party member. In addition, at a meeting of the Comintern and Profintern held on 26 July, 900 million francs was allocated from Soviet sources and 100 million from other countries. The republic even approached Germany for arms against cash but the request was politely shelved. A number of pilots and technicians were recruited in France, and some Russians appeared in Republican Spain late in August to help organize aid and resistance.

The political moves to help either side in the conflict were complicated by several factors. In England, although private groups did their best to send aid, the government under Stanley Baldwin was determined to maintain strict neutrality. Germany had no wish to get involved in any possible European conflict by provoking any Soviet or French reaction by giving public support, so initially military supplies were sent secretly, the German Foreign Office being left unaware of Hitler's action until some time in October. France was under pressure from Britain to come out in favour of non-intervention, this move being backed up on 7 August by the threat that if France persisted in her supplies and war followed, Britain would not come to her aid as arranged under the Locarno Treaty. The next day the French Cabinet closed the frontier and declared their support of non-intervention in the teeth of enthusiastic popular backing for the Republic. Stalin was busy liquidating the group known as the

58

'Old Bolsheviks' and did little beyond giving permission for some financial aid until late in September, when the first shipments of tanks, planes, munitions, vehicles, tank crews, and pilots were made. Italy was openly sending help in the form of planes and pilots, and it would not be long before she also sent troops. Thus in the first two or three months of the war there was much official support for non-intervention covering a great deal of aid to both sides. It is not surprising that when British efforts to limit the Civil War culminated in the formation of a Non-Intervention Committee, that body should have had a chequered and difficult career. However, it did come into being and met in London on 9 September with every European country represented except Switzerland which remained rigidly neutral to everything. It began its work typically by discussing what procedure to adopt. The Committee did very little to affect the immediate course of the fighting as it was dominated by the Great Powers who, apart from Britain and France, continued to act as their interests demanded.

Back in Madrid, the gravity of the situation was obvious. Slightly earlier a daring attempt to retake Majorca had failed when a Catalan-Valencian force, which had landed on the north-east coast on 16 August, was thrown out on 3 September by a counter-attack covered by Italian aircraft. The Republicans had managed to destroy resistance at Gijón in the north, but Oviedo still held out. The Prime Minister, José Giral, faced a crisis due to his failure to get weapons from France, and his lack of dynamic quality. Not surprisingly, he resigned on 4 September and President Azaña approached Largo Caballero, who had been working tirelessly to keep the war going efficiently. After consultation with the Anarchists, who refused to join any government, he took office on the understanding that he could include some Communists in his Cabinet. He also took over the War Ministry himself. Army discipline was tightened up and its political motivation was strengthened by the appointment of Commissars, whilst the first steps were taken to incorporate the various militia groups effectively into the Republican armies.

61   Largo Caballero – a photo taken on a visit to the siege of the Alcázar at Toledo

On the other side, General Franco had been gaining in reputation with the result that the rebel (now Nationalist) council appointed him Supreme Commander on 12 September. Then, by a decree of 29 September, they gave him the position of Head of Government. But when the decree appeared in print the word 'state' had been substituted for 'government' – Nicolás Franco, the General's brother, had instructed the printer to make the change unknown to the other generals. The Army Staff, the Falangists, and the Carlists had been outwitted, and the once almost unknown officer of the Army of Africa was now the 'Caudillo' of all Nationalist Spain.

The new leader moved his headquarters to Salamanca. General Varela and four army columns awaited his order to advance. On 6 October all was ready and the attack began with a drive northwards which was designed to link up with a thrust from Ávila which at first met stiff resistance in the Sierra de Gredos. General Yagüe returned to duty to take command directly under Varela and the advance began again with the opposing militia forces being broken and then machine-gunned from the air as they pulled back towards Madrid. General Mola was optimistic enough to say jokingly that he would be at a café in the Gran Vía in the heart of the capital enjoying a cup of coffee there on 12 October. The waiters at one of the cafés kept his table reserved for him when he failed to appear on the due date!

The danger was now very near. Largo Caballero called up more conscripts but refused to order the construction of defence works. Elsewhere, Oviedo was relieved on 16 October, and the next stage of the Madrid attack coincided with this event. A general advance began to the north, whilst a new thrust from the south got to Illescas on 17 October. President Azaña retired to Barcelona leaving the Premier and Cabinet to their own devices. Potential Fifth Columnists were hunted out and shot. General Miaja was recalled from his enforced retirement and given overall command in Madrid.

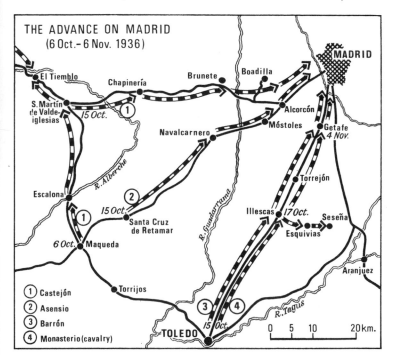

MAP 4
THE ADVANCE ON MADRID.
The attack was carried out by the Army of Africa under General Varela (second-in-command Colonel Yagüe). Phase 1: Castejón moves north (6 October) from Maqueda to link up at El Tiemblo with the Avila column under Valdés Cabanillas. Phase 2: Four columns move up (15 October) main roads to west side of Madrid

62   Dolores Ibarruri ('La Pasionaria') speaking at a rally

63   Bombed houses near Toledo

The southern Nationalist thrust swung east to threaten the Valencia road. Enemy gunfire could now be heard in Madrid.

Suddenly new hope came for the Republic. In return for some £65 million in gold, Stalin had ordered arms to be sent and the first supplies arrived at Cartagena on 15 October. Tanks and planes were sent direct to Madrid. The first Russian tank battle took place on 29 October, when the Russian commander, General Pavlov, burst through to Esquivias. He had to withdraw as he lacked supporting infantry, but his unexpected appearance gave the Nationalists a false idea of the strength of the defences to the south of the capital. But in spite of this temporary relief, the end seemed to be near. General Mola evidently thought so, for he moved down to Ávila and assumed command for the great attack.

The preliminary air bombing began on 29 October and the columns moved steadily nearer so that Getafe and its aerodrome fell on 4 November and the first out-lying suburbs were reached next day. Madrid was tense and crowded with refugees, with General Miaja trying to do what he could to meet the coming siege. The government was widened by the inclusion of Anarchists at long last. At first light on 8 November the artillery began the onslaught to cover a triple drive from the west up the slope above the little river Manzanares; a feint attack was also planned to move forward in the southern suburb of Carabanchel and to make towards the Toledo Bridge.

Madrid seemed to be doomed. In fact Lisbon Radio broadcast a brilliant description of Franco entering the city on a white charger! But thousands of militia, soldiers, and workers were massing to meet the oncoming regulars. That famous Communist, Dolores Ibarruri ('La Pasionaria') kept broadcasting to the defenders urging them on;

64 General Kléber (Lazar Stern), one
of the International Brigade commanders

65 Republican propaganda card which
carried the slogan *They shall not pass*

barricades were hurriedly put in place; morale rose again. The Premier and government had abandoned the city on 6 November and General Miaja was nominally in
control. But real power now lay with the Communists and the planning of resistance
was actually being done by the Russian General Gorev. The Nationalist drive was
temporarily blunted.

A new force now made its weight felt in the struggle. A few weeks earlier, the
Comintern had begun setting up an organization to recruit and train foreign volunteers,
these to be incorporated in battalions according to nationality and organized into an
International Brigade. As the Nationalists regrouped for a fresh attack in the afternoon
of 8 November, a long column of well-disciplined men marched along the Gran Vía.
The XIth International Brigade under its Hungarian commander Lazar Stern, known
as General Kléber, was moving to take up position to the west of Madrid. The slogan
of the madrileños – 'no pasarán' – 'they shall not pass' – suddenly acquired fresh
meaning, for although the Brigade was less than 2,000 in number, it comprised high-
class and determined troops, and put heart into the men who had stopped the first
attack. Varela was forced to turn his feint attack into the real thing, but the narrow
streets of Carabanchel were an ideal defence system, and his Moroccans had had no
training in street fighting. Kléber then counter-attacked to the west of the Manzanares,
losing over 500 men but pushing back the Casa de Campo attackers. The bombing
increased, high explosive and incendiaries being dropped to create fires. But Madrid

did not panic as expected and the air raids had the effect of stiffening the will of the population to resist. So when the XIIth International Brigade arrived on 12 November, it was sent to cover the road to Valencia. It reached its sector, weary from a long march, to be attacked almost at once. Confusion in orders and lack of artillery support hampered its mobility and it was pulled back into Madrid.

Durutti, the Anarchist leader, had also arrived with a strong force, and Miaja used these fresh troops to reinforce the Casa de Campo sector. When the Anarchists went into the attack on 15 November they came under accurate and intense machine-gun fire and refused to go on. Varela then struck at them, and after fierce fighting, the Anarchists fled. The Moroccans swarmed up the hill into the new University City to the north-west corner of Madrid, whilst the remnants of the XIth Brigade were flung in to meet them. After ferocious hand-to-hand fighting both sides were exhausted and dug themselves in, the Nationalists having captured some two-thirds of the University site.

Madrid now began to suffer the full horrors of heavy bombing as the newly created German Condor Legion planes moved in. Shells fell on the western and central areas from the Casa de Campo direction. Thousands left for the eastern provinces. Durruti was killed on 20 November. The foreign embassies moved out. But the great attack which was to bring Madrid to its knees had ended in stalemate. General Mola's chair still awaited him in the Gran Vía.

66   Pilots of the German Condor Legion 'scrambling'

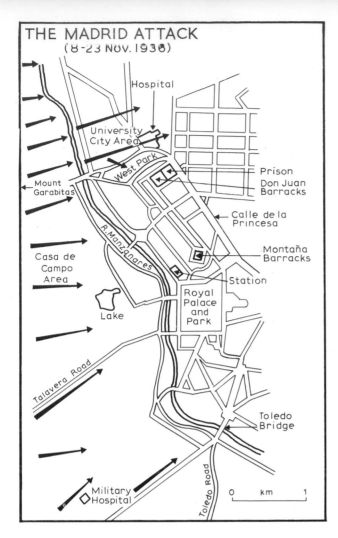

THE MADRID ATTACK
(8-23 Nov. 1938)

Hospital

University
City Area

West Park

Mount
Garabitas

Casa de
Campo
Area

R. Manzanares

Lake

Prison
Don Juan
Barracks

Calle de la
Princesa

Montaña
Barracks

Station

Royal
Palace
and
Park

Talavera Road

Toledo
Bridge

Military
Hospital

Toledo Road

0   km   1

MAP 5
THE MADRID ATTACK. Phase 1:
Thrust in the centre to take the
Montaña Barracks. Phase 2:
Attempted breakthrough in
Carabanchel sector to south-west.
Phase 3: Successful push into the
University City on north-west
fails to penetrate further.
Nationalist Commander: Varela
with 20,000 men of the Army of
Africa, and German and Italian
tanks and air support.
Republican commanders: Miaja,
Rojo, Kléber, with militia and
Russian tanks and aircraft. The
Russian General Gorev was a key
figure in the planning of defence
operations. The arrival of the XIth
and XIIth International Brigades
effectively blocked any further
attacks and the battle ended in a
stalemate

67   Open-air mass in the Sierra Nevada,
October 1936

64

7 The Two Spains

THE CIVIL WAR had now been going on for four months. The initial risings had led not to the expected quick victory but to a full-scale conflict, which had drawn in foreign troops and volunteers and had even threatened the possibility of a European war. The rebels were now a firmly established alternative government and had begun to call themselves Nationalists. The Republicans, though still ideologically divided amongst themselves, were in the process of creating some sort of unified military command and a more or less effective central government system. Spain had become two countries of opposed political structure and character.

In the Nationalist Zone the pattern of government was basically military and had been so since 24 July when Mola had set up a *junta*, or council, in Burgos with General Cabanellas as its nominal President. The original council members were four generals, Mola, Dávila, Ponte, and Saliquet, and two colonels, Montaner and Moreno. The President and the two junior members formed the administrative branch. General Franco was brought into the council in August. Mola was in charge of the northern area, Franco controlled Morocco, whilst a non-council man, Queipo de Llano ran Andalusia and provided a nightly propaganda talk on Seville Radio full of threats, vituperation, and vulgar jokes, which made him one of the most celebrated broadcasters in Europe! Day-to-day administration was carried on by hundreds of civilian volunteers in the absence of any proper civil service. Justice was very sketchy at the start but soon a system of military tribunals was set up in place of the usual civil courts. Such was the zone which General Franco was ultimately to control as he gained in power and influence, becoming Supreme Commander on 12 September and Head of State from 1 October.

Nationalist Spain was thus essentially a military state in which civilians occupied the second place. There were no political parties as such apart from the Falange, the original political wing of the movement. With its leader, José Antonio, in a Republican gaol and few of its original members still alive, it quickly lost its position, a vast influx of new members who joined to show their patriotism reducing it to a shadow of its former dynamic self. The Carlists, who formed a movement rather than a political party in the accepted sense of the word, had been sidetracked by Mola, and their leader, Manuel Fal Conde, managed to cross General Franco's path and was exiled to Portugal for a time at the end of 1936. Even if politically these two groups had no real influence, they did provide a considerable number of fanatical and courageous troops to aid the Nationalist movement. Outside such political groups, the church hierarchy was solidly in support of the generals, though this solidarity decreased as one went down the scale. In certain areas numbers of priests were pro-Republican in their sympathies. Outwardly, Nationalist Spain presented an appearance of unity, though tensions and rivalries existed beneath the surface.

As the rising developed from a rebellion against anarchy into a crusade fought under the old Monarchist flag of Spain for the protection of Christendom, a more pressing problem was the economic one. Nationalist Spain had little enough financial backing at the start; the country's gold reserve – the fourth highest in the world – was in Republican hands, and the occupied area was not a source of immediate wealth. By cutting expenditure, imposing higher taxes, and slowing down debt payments, something was done to meet needs. The peseta rate had been pegged at its pre-war level but had nothing to back it except hope. But even so, the Nationalist rate was always higher than that for the Republican peseta. For one thing the Germans had set up a trading agency to cover the movement of their military aid (HISMA – 'The Hispano-Moroccan Transport Company'). In return Spanish raw materials passed through this agency so that her metal products and some food items were sent to Germany and used as payment for arms. This 'trade' did help to stabilize things to some extent, and further stability grew from the general hope of foreign traders and financial circles that Nationalist Spain would win. It was true that foreign investments had been scrupulously respected hitherto, but if the Republic began copying Russia's example, all would be lost. So in spite of some friction between General Franco and his various allies, his zone was financially viable internationally, so that such things as vital oil supplies could be obtained. The Texas Oil Company became the main supplier and delivered just under 2 million tons during the war in spite of being fined for breaking the Embargo Act of the United States.

At the outbreak of war, the Republic was under the Presidency of Manuel Azaña, with Casares Quiroga of the Republican Left party as Prime Minister. The main political problem was that of preserving a balance between three powerful groups, the Socialists, Anarchists, and Communists, who at times were just as likely to attack each other as they were ready to resist the common enemy. On the 18 July Casares Quiroga had found himself trapped by circumstances. The news from Morocco and parts of Spain was confused – the Madrid workers were angrily demanding weapons – there seemed to be no way of controlling either the rising or the government supporters. The Prime Minister resigned in despair. Next day José Giral, a former Navy Minister, took over with the tacit approval of the three main political groups. Orders were given to

68   Republican propaganda postcard of 1937 caricaturing the elements in the Nationalist Junta of Burgos. Note the gallows, where Spain is being squeezed to death

69   [*opposite*] Burgos October 1936. General Franco accompanied by General Cabanellas on the way to his investiture as Chief of State

66

distribute arms and some sort of military preparedness was planned. In spite of these actions, the new government was still basically middle class liberal in tone, but the real strength of Republican resistance and the real power was in the hands of the Socialists and the Unions in Madrid. When Giral failed to get the aid from abroad which was so desperately needed, it was mainly through the pressure exerted by the Unión General de Trabajadores that he was forced to resign on 4 September, to be replaced by Largo Caballero. In Catalonia a similar situation arose with President Companys as nominal leader but the dominant Anarchists in effective control.

Republican Spain thus had two centres of government, Madrid and Barcelona, each of which was the base for separate military operations, though at times there was some co-ordination of effort and mutual support. Both centres possessed a Head of Government and ministers, but these were not in full control, both being very open to pressure groups which wielded effective power from below. As the war progressed, the extreme left groups became more and more dominant in Madrid, so that the Communist party, though relatively small in numbers, played an increasingly important part. As a result of its dynamic attitude to the war the party gained members, and did its best to increase its influence by working its way into the government and by playing off the various Socialist groups against each other in order to weaken any opposition. Gradually the overall power of the Socialists in Madrid and of the Anarchists in Catalonia was undermined as the Communist plan of 'Divide and rule' was put into effect.

Throughout the war, these struggles for power continued to hamper any attempts to form one central body for the control of the fighting and of administration. Largo Caballero had tried to set up a Supreme War Council early in November with three other ministers, but it hardly ever met and did little good. However, another committee in Catalonia, which was organized to plan arms production, was a success, and by the end of 1936 was producing results efficiently.

67

With all the tensions and urgent problems which faced Republican Spain, Largo Caballero and his government had more than enough to do. But in spite of all these preoccupations, much was done in areas not directly connected with the war. Money was found for education, so that more schools could be opened. The medical services were also improved. Local government was brought back under government control by the restoration of a more normal municipal system. The many local tribunals, some known as *checas* after the Russian revolutionary courts, were replaced by Popular Tribunals on a sounder legal basis. Women were given legal rights they had not previously enjoyed. The government's aim was clearly to try to stabilize the country by means of properly constituted institutions which it alone would control.

In agriculture something of a revolution was brought about in several ways, the chief of which were the setting up of village collectives in which all who worked the fields received according to their needs in a closed community, and the big increase in the number of tenant farmers due to the redistribution of land which had been ex-propriated from its former Nationalist owners. The Republican rural areas thus changed radically in character in a matter of a few months.

But underneath it all, the basic divisions still remained. In the Nationalist zone some sort of unity could be imposed from above. But in the Republican area neither Largo Caballero nor anyone else had the necessary physical power to enforce unity. In the fighting areas some sort of military unified command did evolve as an efficient solution to the problems of the battlefield. Back in the rear areas, away from the very real danger presented by an enemy close at hand, any unification was a matter of expediency. There was always the possibility that a political truce would turn into a political war overnight. Internal ideological conflicts could destroy Republican Spain just as completely as the Nationalists were seeking to do, and could do so at any moment.

70 Nationalist propaganda postcard showing President
Azaña as Nero. It is entitled: 'Anzaña's historic sentence:
Now the Republic is proclaimed.'

8 War of Attrition

THE MILITARY SITUATION around Madrid became quiet for the next three weeks until the start of a new Nationalist offensive to the north-west on 13 December 1936. The city was now an advanced military fortress under General Miaja (and his Russian allies), with very little effective contact with the civilian government now a safe distance from the fighting in Valencia. During the lull two important events occurred elsewhere in Spain – José Antonio Primo de Rivera was shot and the Basques opened their first and last offensive in the north-east.

José Antonio was tried in Alicante with his brother Miguel and the latter's wife. The Popular Tribunal sentenced the Falange leader to death, but accepted his appeal for clemency for his brother and sister-in-law, who were both reprieved. The sentence was forwarded to Valencia for confirmation, but whilst it was being studied, the Cabinet heard that the execution had already been carried out on 20 November.

The Basque Republic's surprise offensive was aimed at Vitoria, the capital of Álava, and was led by General Francisco Llano de la Encomienda at the head of some 30,000 men, the majority Basque Nationalists. The first stage was an attack on Villarreal de Álava on 30 November, but the town held out long enough for a relief column to reach the area from Vitoria. The weight of Nationalist artillery and air power forced the Basques to pull back on 5 December and the offensive collapsed.

Meanwhile, to the north-west of Madrid the Nationalists had begun probing attacks from their positions due west of the capital in preparation for a drive on towards the road from Madrid to the Escorial Monastery (the Corunna Road). The plan was to develop an offensive to cut the road, then to seal off the western end of the Sierra de Guadarrama, thus rolling back the Republican line in the mountains. The main attack opened on 13 December under General Varela with General Orgaz, as Supreme Commander of the Madrid front, in control. The first objective was the little village of Boadilla, 20 kilometres west of Madrid. It fell on 14 December, but was retaken by the Republicans. Two battalions of the International Brigade occupied it only to be surrounded and suffer heavy casualties. A second offensive just north of Brunete had as its objective the village of Villanueva de la Cañada which was also captured. Over Christmas both sides brought up reinforcements, the Nationalists drawing on their newly opened officer training depot at Cáceres and on their conscripts.

The second phase of the Corunna Road battle opened on 3 January 1937 with two axes of attack, one aimed at Las Rozas on the railway line going north, the other at Pozuelo halfway between Boadilla and Madrid. The first objective was gained on 4 January, but the second column ran into tough opposition. Then on 5 January a new form of tactics broke the Republicans up successfully. This was a rudimentary form of *blitzkrieg*, an experiment for the benefit of the German observers in Spain. The attack opened with aerial bombing, a tank wave followed supported by mobile artillery, infantry came next supported in turn by more tanks. Some of the Republican brigades lost contact with each other, others ran out of ammunition. The advance went steadily on. Reinforcements came from the front south of Madrid, and the XIVth International Brigade was rushed up from Córdoba to stem the tide. A battalion was

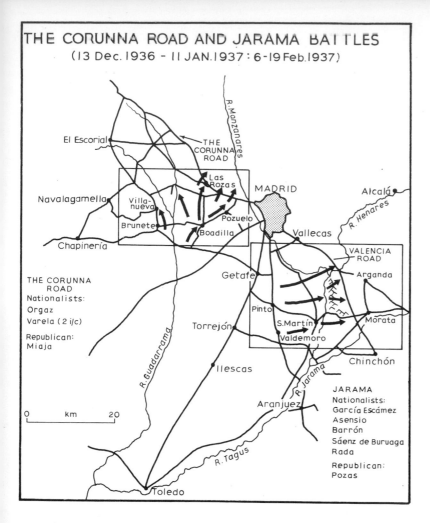

THE CORUNNA ROAD AND JARAMA BATTLES
(13 Dec. 1936 - 11 JAN. 1937 : 6-19 Feb. 1937)

THE CORUNNA ROAD
Nationalists:
Orgaz
Varela (2 i/c)

Republican:
Miaja

0   km   20

JARAMA
Nationalists:
García Escámez
Asensio
Barrón
Sáenz de Buruaga
Rada

Republican:
Pozas

MAP 6
(i) THE CORUNNA ROAD
BATTLE. From a line just
north of Brunete–Villa-
viciosa–Madrid, Varela
pushed out a salient
cutting the road between
Madrid and Las Rozas.
(ii) THE JARAMA BATTLE.
Five columns drove north-
east from the Madrid–
Aranjuez road with the
main Valencia road as
their objective. They
crossed the river Jarama,
but were held up in the
heights to the east. The
nearest point reached to
their objective was the
junction of the Jarama
and Manzanares rivers

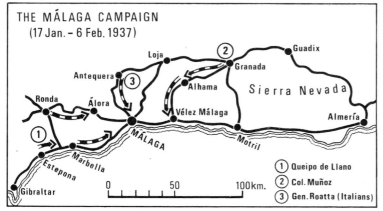

THE MÁLAGA CAMPAIGN
(17 Jan. – 6 Feb. 1937)

① Queipo de Llano
② Col. Muñoz
③ Gen. Roatta (Italians)

MAP 7
THE MÁLAGA CAMPAIGN.
Phase 1 : A column from
Estepona takes the town
of Marbella and one from
Granada takes Alhama.
Phase 2 : The Spanish
forces close on Málaga
while Italian armour
moves south from Antequera

moved up to Las Rozas (the Thaelmann Battalion), where it was surrounded but held
out for two days before being practically destroyed. The Nationalists now held over
10 kilometres of the road, but could get no farther. On 10 January the XIVth Brigade
accompanied by the XIIth arrived at the front. Next day they counter-attacked in

70

terrible conditions with some success, only to be pushed back to their start line. The battle then ended with the Nationalists over the road, but with the Sierra line still firmly held by the Republicans. For nearly a month the Madrid front became calm again, another sector in Andalusia being the centre of military activity.

In the south the Nationalist line now ran from the coast north of Gibraltar up to Ronda then east along the mountain range to a point south-east of Granada. The Republican territory in this area was thus almost indefensible and could only be supplied from outside through Motril. In January 1937 this road was closed by flooding at that town. General Queipo de Llano seized this opportunity, the offensive opening on 17 January with a drive north to Marbella coupled with a similar push south from Granada as far as Alhama. Colonel Villalba, the Republican officer at Málaga, seems to have thought that this was all that his enemies planned. He had some 40,000 militiamen and no problems of morale, but he clearly did not realize that forming up north of Antequera was a formidable force of Italian Black Shirts consisting of tanks, motorized infantry, and armoured cars. This Italian group of nine battalions was a separate military entity under the command of an Italian, General Roatta. It was a real threat to the badly organized but brave defenders of Málaga, who were now on their own as no help was to be sent them from Valencia.

On 3 February the offensive was renewed, first from the west starting from Marbella; some twenty-four hours later the Italian armour began moving on the direct road south to Málaga itself. The front broke under both thrusts. The town was bombed from the air and shelled from the sea, all further resistance now being hopeless. Evacuation was ordered, and all who could fled up the coast road, which had been left uncut on purpose as the Nationalist and Italian forces did not relish the idea of a last ditch defence in the town itself with consequent heavy casualties. The town was entered on 8 February. A large number of Republican supporters were promptly

71   Málaga Campaign early 1937. Nationalist troops at a rest point

71

executed, some without trial. Meanwhile, the pursuers of the fleeing troops and civilians had caught up with them, and more shootings occurred. When the fighting ceased the Nationalists had gained the coastal strip to well past Motril with no serious difficulty. For the Italians, the relatively easy campaign was to lead them to disaster in March 1937, when they came up against a really tough opposition in the battle for Guadalajara. Largo Caballero appears to have decided early on in the offensive that Málaga was not worth reinforcing, especially in view of the greater danger that Madrid would very soon be in the fighting once more. Actually, even before Málaga fell, his attention was violently drawn to the capital and to its precarious situation.

On 6 February, the Republican commander south of Madrid, General Sebastián Pozas, suddenly had to deal with two powerful thrusts in the sector covering the river Jarama. Two columns with artillery support were pushing eastwards, one from just south of Getafe towards a peak dominating the area called La Marañosa, the other having moved up the road from Aranjuez to Ciempozuelos. General Pozas had been thrown off balance by this unexpected offensive as he himself was concentrating troops for an attack westwards. By 7 February a third column to the north had reached the Manzanares tributary, bringing the key road to Valencia under gunfire. From Madrid General Miaja reinforced the danger zone and by next day fresh troops and the original forces in the area were forming a defence line based on the high ground to the east of the Jarama to block any further advance eastwards.

The three key crossing points which were now to be the focal centres of the offensive were, from north to south, the Arganda, Pindoque, and San Martín de la Vega bridges. On 11 February, the Nationalists had forced the first one and a full brigade crossed during the morning to meet one battalion of the International force, which was nearly annihilated. But a second battalion did succeed in blocking the way to Arganda itself. In the centre, the Pindoque bridge had also been seized after Moroccans had knifed the guards just before dawn, and an attempt to blow it up had

72 Aragón sector. A typical machine-gun in action (in the hands of two Republican soldiers)

73 A member of the P.O.U.M., apparently wearing British web equipment

74   Casa de Campo 1936. Poster commemorating a Republican hero Seaman Coll, who personally destroyed four Nationalist tanks

75   General Miaja in Madrid

76   Action picture of a soldier hit by a bullet

failed. Here, however, intense fire from the heights to the east contained the bridge-head. A third attack at the southern end of the salient had resulted in the capture of San Martín de la Vega but here the bridge was still held until nightfall. Once more, the guards were knifed and the Nationalist brigade concerned then advanced to take the high ground known as Pingarrón. A second brigade followed up this success so that the advance was pushed on in the direction of Morata de Tajuña on the river Tajuña. Fierce fighting now developed in this sector as the British Battalion of the XVth Brigade strove to block the advance, suffering 375 casualties out of a strength of 600 in so doing. But the slight Nationalist gain at this point was balanced by a retreat in the north where the second brigade in the attack had been pushed back to the Jarama. There were hardly any reserves left to throw in; the Republicans had command of the air with Russian fighter cover, and Russian tanks were now stiffening the defenders' resistance.

There was a temporary decrease in the intensity of the battle for a day, which gave General Miaja an opportunity to review the position. He assumed overall command, and brought all the forces in the area under one unified group known as 3rd Army Corps. Four International Brigades held a continuous defensive line east of the river (XIth, XIIth, XVth, XVIIIth). On 17 February, Miaja ordered a counter-attack which made a little progress in the northern sector, but ran into trouble in the southern one where casualties were heavy, the American Battalion of the XVth Brigade losing nearly 300 men out of 550. When the battle died down both sides dug in. Forty-five thousand dead and wounded had resulted from the struggle, the Republicans losing 25,000. The Valencia road was still open, though the Nationalists had created a salient 15 kilometres deep almost up to it.

This battle, which was almost a military setpiece, illustrates some general points

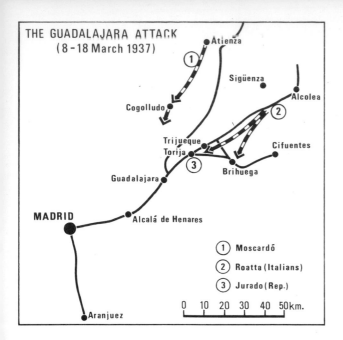

MAP 8

THE GUADALAJARA ATTACK.
Moscardó (1) was to cover the
right flank of the main thrust
under Roatta (2) who had 250
tanks and air cover. He was
stopped by 4th Army Corps under
Jurado (3). His retreat was turned
into a rout by air attacks flown
from Barajas when his own aircraft
were grounded by bad weather. A
supporting thrust from the Jarama
sector failed to materialize

in its conduct and its results. The initial plan of the Nationalists was strategically sound
with its five columns and its close support by artillery. But the fact that it lost control
of the airspace over the battlefield was an adverse factor in that it also lost the valuable
help which bombing can give in this type of terrain. The second important factor
which prevented full development of the attack was one which continually hampered
Nationalist commanders – the lack of reserves at crucial moments. It is not uncommon
in battles of a limited nature of the type of the Jarama one that there comes a point in
the fighting where one more attack by fresh troops will turn a stubborn but tiring
defence into a breakthrough. It is quite possible that such a build up of the thrust up
the road to Morata might have turned the Republican left flank and enabled the
Nationalists to catch the defence from the rear. However, it must be said here that the
Republican forces put up a fierce and often intelligent resistance. After the inexplicable
blunder they committed by not ensuring the complete destruction of the three key
bridges, they succeeded in containing a very dangerous threat by making the Nationalists fight for their gains all the way. Although the battle was in some sense a defeat as
the Nationalists had advanced to quite a depth, the effect on Republican morale was to
give it a much-needed boost. The one serious outcome of the fighting for the Republicans
was that their losses were not only heavier than those of the Nationalists, they were
suffered by some of their best fighting troops, the International Brigades. Replacements
of a similar quality would be hard to obtain.

But this consideration was outweighed by the effect of a real victory for the
Republicans. There was no doubt that their troops won the next big battle in the
Madrid area, the struggle for Guadalajara, a key town to the north-east of the city,
fought between 8 and 18 March. This offensive, which was to provide the Italians with
a glorious victory, ended for them in an ignominious rout.

The overall plan was a sound one in theory, and was first put forward whilst the
Jarama battle was still being fought. The main idea was to capture Guadalajara, then
swing south to Alcalá de Henares following the river valley. General Orgaz was to push
forward from the Jarama front to effect a link-up at Alcalá. The final objective thus

74

was the complete encirclement of Madrid. It was an attractive plan – if it worked. The concentration of area for the forces involved was just south of Sigüenza, the initial line-up being, from west to east: General Moscardó in command of 20,000 Spanish troops of the Legion, Moroccans, and a contingent of Carlists, then an Italian army 30,000 strong. Moscardó was to protect the Italian right flank and push southwards as they advanced down the main axis of attack, the Saragossa–Madrid road. The result, if all went well, would be a roughly triangular salient, the apex being Guadalajara, the east side the river Tagus, and the west the river Henares. The Italians were commanded by General Roatta who had under him General Bergonzoli (Littorio Division), General Coppi (Black Flames), General Nuvolari (Black Arrows), and General Rossi (Black Shirts). The force disposed of some 250 tanks with artillery support and air cover supplied by two squadrons of fighters operating from nearby temporary airfields. The Republican defence line was held by two untried divisions with Russian fighter cover based on the aerodrome at Barajas near Madrid.

Just after dawn on 8 March the offensive started with an immediate success. General Coppi broke the main defences open, whilst to his right Moscardó made a similar gap. But suddenly the weather changed and it began to rain steadily, the Nationalist aircraft being grounded as a result. On the Jarama front similar weather prevented General Orgaz from getting his attack going either so the southern pincer of the plan failed to operate. On 9 March Coppi began advancing once more then swung left whilst Nuvolari came into his place. Keeping pace with them Moscardó

77 Italian tanks in action, a still from the film,
To Die in Madrid

took Cogolludo on the right. The salient grew in depth so that by dawn next day the Italians had seized Brihuega.

The Republicans resorted to the same system which had proved effective on the Jarama front – regiments and units of all kinds were formed into the 4th Army Corps under Colonel Jurado. Some of the troops had in fact come across from the other front, as, for example, the XIth International Brigade which now formed part of the 11th Division commanded by Enrique Lister, a Communist who had considerable military talent, or the XIIth now in a group led by an Anarchist, Cipriano Mera. The two divisions were drawn up in the form of a letter 'V', covering the junction of the Cifuentes and Torija roads with the main highway. Amongst the battalions from the XIIth Brigade was an Italian one, the Garibaldi. This battalion began to move towards Brihuega, in complete ignorance of the fact that the town had fallen a few hours earlier. On the way a forward patrol was met by a single scout from the Black Flames Division, who asked the way to Torija. He was told in Italian, thought that his informants were from General Nuvolari's Division, and rode back on his motor cycle to his lines with his information. General Coppi received his report and began to move down the road to Torija thinking that his fellow general was moving parallel to him. His troops ran right into the Garibaldi Battalion with fatal results. In fact Nuvolari and his Black Arrows were moving; they were smashing their way through Lister's 11th Division and in the process of taking Trijueque. The reconstituted Thaelmann Battalion suffered heavily in trying to block the route south. But on 12 March the pressure was relieved as planes from Barajas began strafing and bombing the Italians. At this point the counter-attack began headed by Russian tanks with Lister's men in close support. Soon the Republicans had live evidence of regular Italian intervention in the shape of numerous prisoners of war. The battle continued on the next two days, the two Italian reserve divisions being roughly handled also by the Republican troops and being pushed back with the divisions they tried in vain to reinforce.

After a lull of nearly seventy-two hours, the full counter-offensive began on

78 Guadalajara 1937. Italian postcard
'commemorating' units fighting in the battle

79 Guadalajara. Italian infantry
advancing in heavy rain

80 Catalan postcard urging all fit men to go to the front

18 March, with an air and artillery bombardment on Brihuega. The defending Italians retreated, their withdrawal becoming almost a rout under the attacks from the air and with their transport in difficulties owing to the muddy conditions on the roads. They had gained no glory but had lost 2,000 dead. Moscardó had done what he was ordered to do and his losses amounted to little more than a handful killed. In fact, Guadalajara is an almost perfect example of how *not* to conduct a *blitzkrieg*, but of all the military experts of Europe very few saw that the failure was not due to any fault in the tactics involved but resulted from the lax execution of the manœuvre. Most of the observers who did see the reality behind the defeat were German. But the Germans always had a low opinion of the Italian professional soldier.

The whole area round Madrid was now quiet and remained so for some three months, the inactivity having a bad effect on the discipline and morale of the members of the International Brigade who had ample time to grumble at the conditions they were experiencing. Desertions increased, drunkenness was a problem and incurred harsh punishment, supplies were often short, and food was generally poor. But a fairly constant flow of volunteers from Eastern European countries at least kept the numbers up even if the fighting strength of the Brigade was not what it had been.

Once again, the Republic had succeeded in meeting and this time inflicting a severe defeat on a theoretically powerful attacking army. The amalgamation of units into one fighting force under one field commander was proving its worth as a solution to the military problem of keeping control of a fluid battle. One can sense a feeling of professionalism, as it were, in the manner in which subordinate commanders dealt

81   Guadalajara 1937. Italian prisoners of war

with situations confronting them. Even if there was a crisis such as a breakthrough it
was met by appropriate action.

The Nationalist High Command must have studied the reports of both the Jarama
and Guadalajara battles with concern, because it was becoming more and more
obvious that plans would now have to be made for what could be a long war. Territory
had been won in both cases, but at a considerable cost in manpower and ammunition.
The effect on morale was bound to be adverse. It was therefore essential to do two
things as quickly as possible – a resounding victory must be won, and the supply of
trained officers and men must be speeded up. If the victory brought with it the winning
of mineral resources, industrial areas, and arms factories, so much the better. The
obvious area which would yield such results was the still Republican north with its coal
and iron, and its iron foundries at Bilbao. The next Nationalist campaign would have to
be designed to capture Asturias and the Basque Provinces. In the meantime the training
of potential officers and non-commissioned officers was put on to a war footing under
General Orgaz, who was a very able and efficient officer and whose training camps
soon began to turn out large numbers of good quality leaders. A large number of the
instructors were Germans, which meant that the standard of training was high. These
military academies produced some 56,000 officers in all, and were an important factor
in the final success of the Nationalist campaigns. The total force eventually under arms
was not far short of 400,000 officers, N.C.O.s, and men. What had begun as a military
rising to be completed in six months had become a war of attrition which might go on
for years.

9 Divide and Rule

IN MILITARY AND POLITICAL CONFLICTS the victor is not infrequently the contestant who has succeeded in weakening the opposition by either inducing or taking advantage of some internal split. Such a success can result either from treachery, defection, or the astute playing-off of one group against another. The two series of events recounted now show all these active in both spheres. The success of the campaign against the Basques and General Franco's assumption of the political leadership of the Nationalist zone both demonstrate the validity of the old maxim: divide and rule.

In the Basque Provinces the result of previous military activity had been the establishment of a corridor from Navarra, a corridor which ran along the French frontier to the north-east and to a short distance west of the river Deva on a line Deva–Vergara–Villarreal from which town the Nationalist line swung west. The main objective of a campaign starting from this line would thus be the port and iron-producing area of Bilbao on the river Nervión. There was an apparently strong defence chain based on the mountains round Bilbao, which was known as the 'Iron Ring'. In between this and the Nationalist zone was a complicated system of mountains and valleys, the main valley being that of the Nervión itself which rises some 8 kilometres west of Vergara. The terrain is such that a determined and well-planned defence could exact very high casualties from any attacker, the defenders' one disadvantage being a shortage of suitable airfields. In theory therefore an attack on Bilbao from the east and south was a potentially dangerous manœuvre. But the Nationalists had one or two fortunate advantages. Firstly, the Basques could expect little help from their comrades of Santander or Asturias, who were largely Anarchists and so loth to aid the staunchly Catholic Basques. Secondly, any reinforcement of the area by sea would be hazardous as the Nationalists were now patrolling the Bay of Biscay. Thirdly, and perhaps most important of all, General Mola had a very good idea of the real strength and the weak points of the defence system, which had been revealed to him by Major Antonio Goicoechea, a former Basque officer who had deserted shortly before.

In preparation for the campaign, General Mola received all the artillery and planes available. His troops were the 61st Division of Navarra (commander General José Solchaga), this being a complete division of 50,000 men. They were deployed from Vergara to Villarreal to form the centre of the attacking force, and were flanked to right and left by the Italian 23rd March Division and a composite Hispano-Italian formation which bore the name of a former wholly Italian unit, the Black Arrows. They had adequate artillery and good air cover with the German squadrons of Heinkels and Junkers, some Italian units, and planes of the Spanish Air Force. Facing them were some 45,000 Basques with few planes and guns and only a dozen tanks. The commander of this force was the general commanding the Republican Army of the North, Francisco Llano de la Encomienda, who had led the ill-fated offensive of November–December 1936.

The attack began with a steady general advance in the direction of Bilbao on 31 March and the dive-bombing of Durango, an important road and rail junction about 11 kilometres behind the front. The left flank ran into very stiff resistance at the

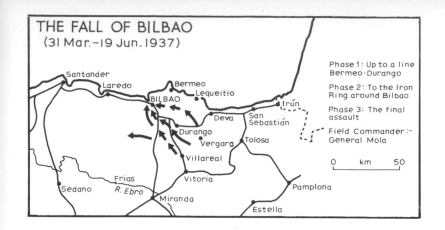

THE FALL OF BILBAO
(31 Mar.–19 Jun.1937)

Phase 1: Up to a line Bermeo-Durango

Phase 2: To the Iron Ring around Bilbao

Phase 3: The final assault

Field Commander:- General Mola

0   km   50

MAP 9

THE FALL OF BILBAO.
On 31 March 1937 Mola
began an advance on
Bilbao from the east and
south-east. The Basques
fell back on the 'Iron
Ring' defences round the
city. The Nationalists
broke through and took
Bilbao on 19 June

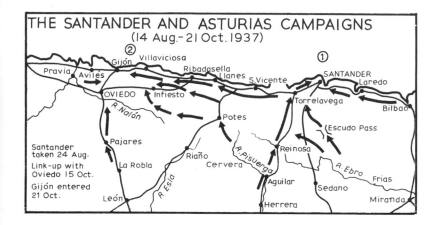

THE SANTANDER AND ASTURIAS CAMPAIGNS
(14 Aug.–21 Oct.1937)

Santander taken 24 Aug.
Link-up with Oviedo 15 Oct.
Gijón entered 21 Oct.

MAP 10

THE SANTANDER AND
ASTURIAS CAMPAIGNS.
On 14 August 1937 a
three-pronged assault on
Santander was launched
on an arc from Bilbao to
Reinosa; the town fell
twelve days later. On 1
September a new advance
began into Asturias which
was cleared by the end of
October, though guerrilla
fighting went on for some
five months

village of Ochandiano which was constantly bombed whilst attackers tried to force their way round on either side of it. By 4 April the ring was nearly closed, so the Basques pulled back, but the weather prevented any close pursuit as rain began falling heavily. Mola regrouped whilst the Basques made new defensive positions further back. As in the case of Málaga, the central government seems to have largely abandoned the Basques to their fate, though General Gorev, who had played an important part in the defence of Madrid, did arrive to advise on the best method of meeting the Nationalist onrush.

Before the offensive was renewed on 20 April, trouble arose over the Nationalist threat to blockade the north coast. As British ships were carrying most of the cargoes involved, this news led to angry exchanges in Parliament and the British government's refusal to escort merchant ships beyond the 3 mile limit. Apparently Mr Baldwin, the Prime Minister, was convinced that information reaching him from the navy on the stringency of the blockade was correct. In fact, on 20 April, the very day the fighting was renewed, a cargo vessel, the *Seven Seas Spray*, got into Bilbao without meeting either Nationalist ships or mines. After one or two arguments between Spanish and British warships, other vessels followed her in. The blockade was largely an astute bluff.

The second phase of the offensive began with the usual bombardment. The Basque forces waiting to receive the first infantry attack suddenly heard the sound of machine-gun fire to the rear. As before, they pulled back to avoid encirclement except round Elgeta, a village well protected by a good trench system. The Nationalists were temporarily halted. But amongst the defending forces were two battalions of the Confederación Nacional de Trabajo and these suddenly left the front without warning. The front crumbled at once, and by 24 April Elgeta had to be abandoned in confusion. On 26 April the Germans, apparently acting on their own initiative, delivered a terror raid on the ancient town of Guernica to the north, practically destroying it though not damaging the famous tree of the Basques. It has never been satisfactorily ascertained

82 [*opposite*] Pablo Picasso's painting *Guernica* (on loan by the artist to the Museum of Modern Art, New York)

83 An Italian Savoia 81 dropping bombs with a Fiat CR 32 fighter escort

if the raid was due to lack of experience or was a deliberate attempt to annihilate a centre of communications. It may also have been an experiment to study the effect of concentrated bombing. In any case, the town was soon captured so that by 30 April the new front ran from Bermeo on the coast, through Guernica, to just west of Durango, then south-west through the mountains. The Iron Ring was some 7 kilometres away at its nearest point. Bad weather once more halted the Nationalists, so the Republicans took the opportunity to send General Gamir Ulibarri to Bilbao. He was an experienced officer who did much to improve the Basques' position. A supply of anti-aircraft guns also arrived from Czechoslovakia, but that was all.

To attempt a diversion, the Republican government opened two offensives, neither of which did anything to relieve the pressure on Bilbao. The first was aimed at Huesca in Aragón when a Catalan force under General Pozas was thrown back with 10,000 casualties. The second began more successfully when General Walter and the XIVth International Brigade got to La Granja near Segovia before General Varela could stop him. A more serious blow to the Nationalists at this time was the sudden death of General Mola in an air crash on 3 June in mysterious circumstances. His place was taken by General Fidel Dávila, General Gómez Jordana replacing Dávila at the head of the Burgos *junta*.

Almost at once General Dávila renewed the Bilbao offensive, so that on 11 June the bombardment and the advance began again with the day ending with three brigades actually up against the Iron Ring. Next day a violent thrust was aimed at a known weak point, the co-ordination of barrage and tank and infantry attack being such that the Basques lost control of the situation and a gap about a kilometre wide was torn in the last defences before Bilbao, which was now in artillery range. All Basque troops still outside the Ring were brought back inside it. Evacuation to the west of civilians now began, many of the children having already been brought away to England. It looked as if the end was only hours away.

But there was still some resistance to be overcome. A new commander, Colonel Putz, took over the 1st Basque Division and, by 15 June, he had established an inner line of defence. Once more the Nationalists hammered at a weak point; the defenders fled leaving all the bridges over the Nervión intact. Bilbao now came under heavy

84 Basque Campaign.
A blockhouse in the
'Iron Ring' of Bilbao

82

85   Photo taken in Southampton in 1938 during the Aid
for Basque Children campaign

shellfire. By 17 June all the right bank had gone, and the enemy was up to the railway station on the left. Two days later, the city fell. This time very few reprisals were carried out as few troops were sent into the town. The key iron works were in full working order, as were the nearby mines. The first stage of the clearance of the north had taken some weeks longer than expected, but the Nationalists had won both a resounding victory and some invaluable material gains. They had also obtained their revenge for Aguirre's curt refusal to join General Orgaz in the 1931 military plot.

With the fall of Bilbao the military situation was once more presenting a grim picture for the Republicans. The only victory they could put against this disaster was a small one. Ever since the start of the Civil War a small group of under 2,000 rebels had held two mountain tops by Santa María de la Cabeza in the Sierra Morena, and had pinned down over five times their number for months. Supplies came in by parachute so that the officer in charge had food and munitions. He was Captain Santiago Cortés of the Civil Guard. Finally, in the spring a determined effort was made to destroy his outpost by some 20,000 men, with the XIIIth International Brigade amongst them. The defenders were forced to abandon one mountain top and the other one was now violently attacked. Cortés was wounded and died shortly afterwards. On 1 May the end came and the sanctuary of Santa María went up in flames as the Republicans broke in. This tragically heroic siege had one bizarre note. For the dropping of breakable supplies to the defenders, the Nationalists used turkeys as the safest means of ensuring safe landings.

The Basque campaign had been overshadowed by political events in Barcelona as early as the end of April, so that to some extent the attention of many Republicans had been diverted from events in the north. However, before examining this struggle for power, it is necessary to record a very similar though less violent struggle in the Nationalist zone.

83

It will be remembered that General Mola had had some trouble in persuading the Carlists of Navarra to join the rising, and when General Franco brought about Fal Conde's exile in December 1936 for alleged insubordination, the Carlists not unnaturally protested. Their dislike for the Head of State was paralleled by similar feelings which Franco's personal control had inspired amongst a group of Falangists, who had come from the Madrid area. The group decided to study the possibility of amalgamating the Carlists and the Falangists in one organization, a suggestion which Fal Conde accepted. However, the plan broke down as the Carlists could see no way of guaranteeing that they would not lose their identity in the larger body. When General Franco learned of this move, which took place in January and February 1937, he adopted the basic idea and also considered its extension so as to include all other groups and parties in one unified Nationalist party. His thinking was encouraged by a new political figure, his own brother-in-law, Ramón Serrano Suñer, who had just succeeded in escaping from the Republican zone. Suñer had been the leader of the Youth Section of the C.E.D.A., and on his arrival in Salamanca he soon began to develop into the chief Nationalist political theorist. He had a deep antipathy for democracy, so that the type of state which he hoped to create in his theories was completely authoritarian in strict accordance with the traditions of Spain's great past. Clearly only one party was needed in such a state.

After the imprisonment of José Antonio Primo de Rivera a council of seven senior party officers had been set up to run the Falange, its chairman being the senior member, Manuel Hedilla. He was a tremendous worker who had considerable backing in the movement, but he did not like the trend of the ideas of Suñer and the Madrid group which were gaining support amongst many of the newer professional members of the party. His enemies determined to oust him, but the attempt misfired. When the council met on 14 April, Hedilla only received two votes out of seven, but his opponents could not get in because they had been imprisoned as the result of a fight the night before.

86 [*opposite*] Catalonia. Refugees from other parts of Spain being given a meal in Barcelona

87 José Sarrió Calatayud, a Republican pilot, who shot down a German bomber at Cambrils

To resolve the deadlock the full Falange Council met on 18 April, and Hedilla got a majority. But these antics had apparently upset General Franco, so Hedilla's triumph was shortlived. Late on 19 April a decree came out uniting the Falange, the Carlists, and all other parties into one party – with General Franco as the new leader. Mola's reaction was restrained. Hedilla refused the honorary position of chairman of the political committee, and was promptly tried for rebellion and sentenced to death. In fact he was condemned to life imprisonment and was released in 1946. That grey eminence, Serrano Suñer, became the new Secretary-General. In this post he would be most useful to his brother-in-law in that he could carry out the task of damping down any further squabbles without the latter being directly involved. If anything went wrong, he could be easily sacrificed – as in fact he was some years later in 1942, when his strong pro-Axis views became a liability to the Caudillo.

General Franco was now Head of State, Supreme Commander of the army, and leader of the only political organization allowed. For a man who was never involved in politics actively, his record was becoming impressive. Luck had helped with the deaths of Sanjurjo and now of Mola, but there was more to it than luck. General Franco is a Galician and therefore is likely to possess some of the typical features of that group, particularly their quiet shrewdness. It is said that a Galician will always answer a question – with another question. Combined with this wiliness, is experience. General Franco had seen how easy it was to prevent large-scale trouble in Morocco by playing off one chief against another. He was now applying the same idea to Nationalist politics – with marked success.

When he came to power in September 1936, Largo Caballero had seemed to be getting close to the Communists, but he soon began to show that he had no ideas of linking up with them. For the moment he did little to antagonize them, but in the spring of 1937 the Prime Minister took some action to curb their penetration, the political Commissars having their powers severely cut, and the defence council in Madrid with its Communist majority being abolished. At this time, the real director of the Spanish party was not its apparent head, José Díaz, or the internationally famous La Pasionaria – it was Palmiro Togliatti, the very shrewd head of the exiled Italian Communist Party. He now began the task of destroying Largo Caballero. He worked fast, aided by a period of riots in Barcelona with the result that, by the end of May, his enemy had resigned the Premiership and had returned to his former post in his old union, the Unión General de Trabajo.

The Barcelona riots which led eventually to Largo Caballero's resignation originated in a complex political tangle which grew from the enmity between the Anarchists and the Partido Obrero de Unión Marxista (P.O.U.M.), and the Catalan Left (Esquerra) and the fairly recently formed Partido Socialista Unificado de Cataluña (P.S.U.C.). Basically this enmity was between Anarchists and Trotskyist Communists in one group and orthodox Communist sympathizers or active members in the other. On the union side, the Confederación Nacional del Trabajo (C.N.T.) was the major one in Barcelona. It was originally a pro-Comintern organization but was no longer a reliable ally.

Towards the end of April, recriminations and an occasional shooting raised the tension, so that the various groups began stockpiling weapons. The trouble began over an attempt by the Catalan government to take over the Barcelona Telephone Exchange from the control of the C.N.T. on 3 May. Rumour and perhaps deliberate provocation by one or more Nationalist agents increased the tension so that within hours the city was in the throes of a civil war of its own. The Communists themselves supported the government of Companys and fought with the Catalan forces against Anarchist extremists. During a lull on 5 May, there was a Cabinet reshuffle and later that day Companys agreed to receive help from Valencia. Fighting broke out again on the following day, but three warships now arrived with Assault Guards and troops sent by Largo Caballero. A further group followed by road. Order was restored and a miniature revolution had ended.

But the explosion gave the Communists a first class chance to bring down Largo Caballero. The attack on him was made through one of his ministers, Ángel Galarza, who was the Minister of the Interior. Galarza was denounced on the grounds that he should have taken action to deal promptly with the Barcelona situation. By failing to act he had helped the counter revolutionaries. The P.O.U.M. newspaper *Adelante* defended its party's policy by attacking the government. On 15 May the Communist members of the Cabinet argued that the P.O.U.M. should be dissolved, but the Prime Minister refused to do so. They then walked out followed by five other ministers. That left only four Anarchists, the Socialist Galarza, and Anastasio de la Gracia, an old friend of Largo Caballero. Next day the Prime Minister resigned but Azaña persuaded him to stay on. Attempts to form a new Cabinet failed when Largo Caballero refused to co-operate with the Communists who already had a candidate for his post in the shape of Juan Negrín, who had been a very good Finance Minister in Largo Caballero's

88 [*opposite*] *Universal Calendar* – by Juan Genovés, a Spanish artist
whose pictures deal with the confusion and mindless
cruelty of war

original Cabinet of September 1936. Obviously the Communists thought that they could keep their man under their control. At the end of May Negrín took over power. His Cabinet included the two Communists who had walked out on Largo Caballero, Jesús Hernández and Vicente Uribe. The Anarchists refused to join but collaborated, only to find themselves pushed out of their few key positions in organizations like the police. It looked as if Togliatti had triumphed. But he and his comrades had seriously misjudged Negrín, who was quite determined and very ready to show them that he was the man in charge. His personality made him dozens of enemies, but his efficiency and extraordinary skill kept him in power until the end of the Civil War, and he continued as Prime Minister of the Republican Government in exile up to 1945. Perhaps in his case the adage already quoted should be replaced by 'dominate and rule'.

The Communists had gained their first objective, so they turned at once to their second, the liquidation of the P.O.U.M. The initial order came from Alexander Orlov, head of the Spanish section of the N.K.V.D. (People's Commissariat for International Affairs). The Spanish Communists objected to their interference from outside, but the Public Order Chief of Barcelona, Colonel Ricardo Burillo, ordered the closure of the P.O.U.M. Headquarters, the party was banned, and forty members of its central committee were seized. Its head, Andrés Nin, was removed to a secret prison, actually Orlov's own gaol at Alcalá de Henares. Negrín tried to discover what had happened but none of the Spanish Communists knew. Nin was a much tougher person than had been thought as he flatly refused to give himself or his companions away. Orlov saw himself in danger if he could not report any progress in the interrogation, so Nin's murder was planned. Some Germans of the International Brigade pretended to be a rescue group from the Nationalist zone. They broke into his prison, and he was driven away to be shot. His brave conduct had saved nearly all his old friends, but he had not been able to save his party. The Communists had at least been partially successful.

89   The Republican Prime Minister,
Dr Negrín

90   Nationalist postcard showing an
Anarchist charioteer with Republican
ministers as his 'horses'

10 Republican Defeats– Brunete and the North

IN APRIL 1937 A DISPUTE had broken out between some of the officers of the republic's new army backed by Largo Caballero, and the Communists backed by General Miaja. The former wanted to open an offensive in Extremadura, whilst the latter, following a plan put forward by the Russian General Gregori Ivan Kulik, supported a thrust down through Brunete, some 25 kilometres to the west of Madrid, which could be developed into a manœuvre to cut off the Nationalist forces round the north-west of the capital. Nothing happened for the moment, but on 6 July the battle for Brunete eventually began with a violent attack on what was a weakly held sector, so that the initial thrust advanced 10 kilometres very quickly and Brunete was surrounded. The fact that the Nationalists were caught napping did not say much for their intelligence system as the attack had been a matter of public gossip in the Republican zone for some weeks.

As in the other recent battles around Madrid, General Miaja was in supreme command of the two Army Corps involved. The Vth Corps was commanded by Juan Modesto and contained the 11th Division (Lister), 35th Division (Walter), and the 46th (Valentín González 'El Campesino'). The XVIIIth Corps consisted of the 15th Division (Gal), 45th Division (Kléber), and the 69th (Durán) with Colonel Jurado as Corps Commander. The total strength was 50,000, with 150 planes and 128 tanks plus artillery support. Lister's division opened the attack successfully and, after surrounding Brunete, took the village to advance beyond it to the Navalcarnero road. But attacks by other units against key villages such as Quijorna, Villafranca del Castillo, Villanueva de la Cañada, and Villanueva del Pardillo were held. Villanueva de la Cañada did fall on 7 July, but the effect of the failure to clear the other points was that the salient had a narrow base. Instead of concentrating on widening this gap, Miaja pushed more units through it. The resultant confusion was greatly to the advantage of the Nationalists, now under General Varela's command and with large reinforcements arriving hourly. The Condor Legion arrived from the north, additional guns were moved to the front, and three divisions were switched from Guadalajara. These were the 12th (Asensio), 13th (Barrón), and the 150th (Sáenz de Buruaga). Eighteen hours after the first attack Varela had re-formed his front, and next day more troops arrived to thicken up his line. On 9 July El Campesino took Quijorna and two days later the other two key villages had fallen. But the command headquarters of the Nationalists at Boadilla firmly resisted. The loss of the initial impetus was fatal. Now the Republicans were on the defensive, and a few days later the expected counter-attack developed.

On 18 July three Nationalist thrusts gained some ground on both the flanks of the salient and towards Brunete itself. Despite desperate resistance the two flank attacks both broke through, then General Barrón with the 13th Division got to Brunete and drove Lister out on 25 July. The Republicans were left with a territorial gain 5 kilometres deep on a front of about 15, bought at the cost of 25,000 dead, many of whom were veteran troops and therefore difficult to replace. The one Republican massed tank attack, against Villafranca, had been a failure, and what could have been a useful striking force was dispersed in an infantry support rôle. The German tank expert, Colonel Wilhelm von Thoma, did not make a mistake like that and advised Varela to select a point of attack, then throw in all available tanks to be followed by the infantry. This was the German theory of the *Schwerpunkt* which was to prove so successful in France, Russia, and North Africa in the 1939–45 war. Spain was proving to be a most useful testing ground, not only for German war material such as planes and guns, but also for experiments in tactics and battle control. The heavy losses thus inflicted on the Republicans meant that Brunete was really a serious defeat and the effect on morale was considerable, especially amongst the International Brigades, at least one of which refused to go into battle during the fighting and nearly started a mutiny

The next defeat for the Republicans was even more serious, as they not only lost heavily in men and material, they also lost mines and steel production to the enemy. After a short lull when Bilbao had been captured, the campaign for the clearance of the remaining Republican-held territory in the north started up once more. Both sides had been busy regrouping and preparing for the next phase, which was clearly going to be a drive on Santander to the west. The lull had lasted for nearly two months whilst the Nationalists brought in more troops to add to the divisions already in the area. As Santander was a Castilian port, the reinforcements were drawn from volunteers from that province. The Republican forces consisted of five divisions under General Gamir Ulibarri, the main body being the XVth Army Corps (three divisions) with a Basque division and an Asturian one added to it. Apart from a dozen or so Russian fighters, they had only a few out-dated planes and one or two reconnaissance aircraft. The terrain was difficult but not impossible for the attacking army. The route along the coastal plain presents few obstacles, and the approach from the south via Reinosa is

91   Nationalist machine-gunners operating in Irún sector

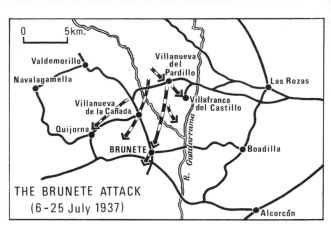

MAP 11
THE BRUNETE ATTACK. The
Russian General Kulik's plan for
a drive south through Brunete to
cut off the Nationalists was put into
effect by Miaja on 6 July 1937. The
initial breakthrough was blocked
by 11 July. A counter-attack came
on 18 July which left a much-
reduced salient only 5 kilometres
deep as the Republican gain

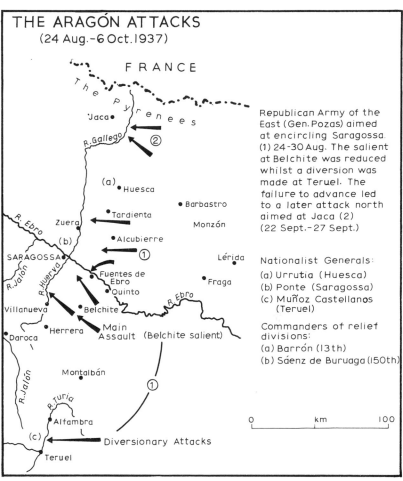

MAP 12
THE ARAGÓN ATTACKS.
The Republican offensive
aimed at Saragossa began
on 24 August 1937 with
three attacks between
Huesca and the Ebro.
Diversionary attacks were
made near Teruel while
the Belchite salient was
driven in. After some
initial success the advance
was contained. At the
north end of the front the
salient protecting Jaca was
reduced in an attack which
began on 22 September

a fairly easy ascent. In between these two there is a more difficult route across the
Escudo Pass. The key to the approaching battle was to be the holding or capture of the
Republican defensive positions on the heights in the Cantabrian mountains.

On 14 August advances began along the coast and up the road to Reinosa. The

92　Republican mountain troops

effect of intensive bombing and shellfire was such that in both sectors the front was smashed, with Reinosa being taken on 16 August. The final blow was the successful storming of the Escudo Pass on 23 August. As many civilians as could find transport or boats fled from Santander. The Basque division withdrew to Santoña where it surrendered to the Italians, who promised safe conduct abroad to them. But before they could leave in the ships which had arrived to take them away, this arrangement was countermanded from Salamanca and they were made prisoners of war. The Nationalists were now on the eastern limits of Asturias.

Before the final phase began, the Republicans opened an offensive in Aragón on 24 August, but as this campaign covers some weeks and thus overlaps the northern battle, it is perhaps more reasonable to conclude the story of that battle before considering the events before Saragossa.

The lull for re-forming was shorter this time. The Santander fighting had not been too exhausting so the Nationalists did not require so much time, and as the enemy was likely to be in some confusion absorbing the troops who had escaped westwards, speed was essential to prevent him consolidating his defences. This was particularly important at this point as the demands of the Aragón front had led to the Condor Legion being transferred there to help in slowing down the initial Republican advance. The Nationalists thus had a powerful infantry and artillery force but no planes to carry out the usual air bombardment which had normally aided them so greatly in the previous mountain campaigns. Fortunately, the opposition amounted to less than 50,000 men in two armies, the XIVth and XVIIth with Colonel Prada in supreme command. The Russian General Gorev was also with the Republicans as adviser. This shortage of manpower tended to counterbalance the better defensive possibilities of the area. In this case, the key pass to the south of Oviedo, the Puerto de Pajares, is a formidable problem for an attacker.

The main weight of the offensive which began on 1 September was thus concentrated on the eastern sector with General Solchaga in command of one army on the coast, and General Aranda leading a second army further inland in the mountains. Without the aid of the Condor Legion to soften up opposition, the progress made was slow. After six weeks' fighting there were still a number of strongpoints held by the Republicans. Solchaga had got as far as Ribadesella on the coast, whilst Aranda had reached the village of Caso about 30 kilometres to the south. Then Aranda swung north in conjunction with a southward push by Solchaga so that the two pincers met at Infiesto. The Republicans panicked and pulled back in headlong retreat to avoid being cut off. The Nationalists followed up fast, and as the Condor Legion had been transferred back to the north, they could now add air strikes to their armoury. The Germans introduced the tactic of 'carpet bombing' at this point, that is, using a tight formation of bombers usually flying at a low altitude which would release their bomb loads simultaneously. The Asturians collapsed under the onslaught; those who could got away, including General Gorev who was eventually picked up by a Russian plane. In Gijón the fifth column of Nationalist sympathizers took the town on 20 October, the main army entering it next day. For some five months guerrilla warfare continued between the Nationalists and nearly 20,000 Republicans who had fled to the mountains, but the end of the campaign meant that the Nationalists now had a sizeable reserve available for use elsewhere, probably consisting of some 30,000 to 40,000 men who could be employed within a short time, with a further 20,000 for use when the

93 General Solchaga

94 Nationalist troops advancing on farm buildings

95   Aragón Front 1937. Republican
troops forming up during the advance of
summer 1937 in the recently captured
village of Quinto

96   The Republican
General Pozas in
September 1937

mopping-up operations against the guerrillas had been completed. They now controlled the coal mines of the north and the iron and steel production of the Bilbao area. Their armies had inflicted over 130,000 casualties on the enemy, of which 33,000 were killed. The extent of the victory may seem surprising in view of the toughness of the fighting elsewhere in Spain. But the Republicans of the north failed to combine together effectively, there was some weakness apparent in the high command, and there was a lack of air cover and tanks. In such circumstances when a breakthrough occurs, its consequences for the defenders are more serious than is normal, as what could be an orderly retreat can swiftly be converted into a confused rout.

The vital importance of keeping firm control of a battle in face of an enemy who has gained some initial advantage is well illustrated by the story of the fighting on the Aragón front at this period. Here the Nationalist line, based on Huesca, Saragossa, and Belchite, was not continuous in that it consisted of a chain of fortified hill positions without interconnecting trenches. Such a line is very vulnerable to a determined thrust unless there is a readily available reserve to be used to seal off the danger point. The Republican decision to open an offensive here is thus strategically sound. But in addition to the strong military reasons for putting such a plan into effect, there were also powerful political ones. Whereas the Anarchists in Barcelona had been effectively removed from power, the Council of Aragón was still firmly under their control under the presidency of Joaquín Ascaso. This independent attitude was a hindrance to the proper prosecution of a centrally run war, so the Communists began to mount an attack. On 11 August Ascaso's Council was dissolved and a Governor-General nominated. To cover this move Lister's 11th Division began to carry out a programme of manœuvres in Aragón. Arrests were made, including those of Ascaso and his Council members. In these circumstances the start of a full-scale attack on the Nationalists in this area could also be conveniently used as a valid excuse to move more troops there in case of trouble caused by any remaining Anarchists or their sympathizers.

The planned offensive was to be carried out by the new Army of the East (the former Catalan Army) under General Pozas. This consisted of five divisions, the 27th under Colonel Trueba, the 45th under General Kléber, and Modesto's Vth Army Corps from the Brunete front (11th, 35th, and 46th divisions), which included four International Brigades. Deployed along the line from the Pyrenees to Teruel, the Nationalists had three divisions with General Urrutia in Huesca, General Ponte the area commander in Saragossa, and General Muñoz Castellanos at Teruel, with one mobile column in reserve under Colonel Galera. Not only did the Republicans have the advantage of surprise, they also outnumbered the Nationalists, at least for a short time.

With no initial bombardment of any kind, multiple attacks began on 24 August in extremely hot weather. The Republican commanders developed a threat to Saragossa by three drives between Huesca and the river Ebro, one of which was directed across the Ebro to put pressure on the Nationalist salient which included Belchite. This push north of the river was to be linked to a second in two attacks south of the river aimed at bypassing Belchite so that the salient could be driven in in preparation for a thrust at Saragossa itself. Minor pushes were planned south of the Belchite sector down to just north of Teruel. This opening met with some success as the Ebro crossing was duly made and on 26 August Mediana had fallen. The sides of the Belchite salient were also pushed back to straighten the line, though the town itself was strongly defended so that some of the Republican forces were held there in a desperate effort to break in. Possibly it was this heroic stand that prevented the full exploitation of the initial gains, because Nationalist reaction was swift and every day's delay was important.

Before any further advance could be begun, Saragossa had received its reinforcements from the Madrid front. General Barrón with the 13th Division halted progress north of the river, whilst Sáenz de Buruaga and the 150th Division tried in vain to

97ʻ Republican priest preparing for Mass on the Basque front

relieve Belchite as the town fell on 6 September. Both sides then dug in and the first phase petered out by mid-September.

The second phase was on a much reduced scale with an offensive aimed at reducing a salient protecting Jaca close to the Pyrenees. Owing to the configuration of the terrain this meant advancing across a river, the Gallego, and over hills and valleys. The battle began on 25 September and lasted some three days, leaving the Republicans established on the west side of the river but no further. Desultory fighting went on for a short period but by 30 September the whole Aragón front had become stable again. The diversionary campaign had not gained a great deal of ground and had little or no effect on the fighting in the north.

Apart from the final clearing of Asturias, the fronts saw little activity until mid-December when the Republicans began a powerful offensive against Teruel, an offensive which began hopefully and which ended in near destruction. As will be seen in a later chapter, this time the Nationalists, in spite of appalling conditions, were able to concentrate such strength in the battle sector that the counter-attacks not only held the Republicans, they destroyed their military supplies and much of their forces. The Aragón campaign had ended in stalemate, the Teruel offensive was to end in severe defeat. But before continuing the account of the military operations, some consideration must be given to the wider aspects of the war up to this point – to the problems of non-intervention and of the Nationalist blockade of the north coast and allied matters. The picture is not complete without some study of the interaction between events in Spain and the policies and conduct of international diplomacy.

98   Action picture showing typical artillery barrage

11 Non-Intervention, Blockade, and Belligerence

BACK IN AUGUST 1936, on an initiative taken by France, Great Britain, Germany, Italy, Russia, and Portugal had supported either by firm signature or by agreement in principle a Non-Intervention Pact which banned all supplies of war materials and men to either side in the Civil War. The idea of thus putting a *cordon sanitaire* round Spain was a logical development of the attempts some of the powers concerned to limit the war and to prevent the possibility of a more generalized conflict arising from it. But Germany and Italy on one side, and Russia on the other, saw it as in their interests to continue to supply aid to their respective allies. So, in spite of the Pact, men, planes, tanks, weapons, and munitions continued to flow into Spain as each accused the other of breaking the agreement and therefore could not stand aside to allow its friends to be defeated because of the other's double-dealing. Not surprisingly some of the meetings of the Non-Intervention Committee set up on 9 September were marked by bitter accusations answered by equally acrimonious diatribes by the accused.

The attitude of the Spanish Republican Government to the Pact was clearly set out in a speech to the League of Nations made by Julio Álvarez del Vayo when the General Assembly met in September 1936. The President had tried to prevent him speaking on the grounds that Spain was not on the agenda, but in vain. The theme of the speech was that the Pact placed the legitimate Republican Government on the same footing as the rebels seeking to destroy it. Under International Law there was no question that his government had the legal right to buy military supplies from abroad, whereas the rebels had no status and were therefore not so entitled.

Then on 10 December Álvarez del Vayo had taken a further step. He succeeded in having the question of Spain placed on the agenda for the next day. When his turn came to speak, he asked the League to condemn both Germany and Italy for their recognition of the rebels, and stressed that the Non-Intervention Agreement was quite useless. The British and French delegates protested that the agreement was having some effect and put forward an alternative plan for mediation. The eventual substantive motion approved by the League asked all members who were also members of the Non-Intervention Committee to do everything possible to ensure that non-intervention was effective, and recommended mediation as a possible solution to the war. Nothing resulted from what was in effect the expression of a pious hope by the League.

Another scheme proved to be more acceptable than mediation or any limitation of volunteers. Lord Plymouth had produced a control plan for the Committee. This envisaged the use of observers to ensure no war materials passed into Spain. The idea was accepted by the Committee on 12 November, and further study was undertaken. The upshot was a more ambitious plan agreed in January 1937. The observers would be stationed round the Spanish frontiers in the bordering countries, and all ships of the Committee members would carry one when bound for Spain. In addition, there would be a naval patrol. Portugal did not approve the plan as she felt it infringed her sovereignty, but the other powers agreed to implement it. Portugal finally agreed to

accept British observers to watch her frontier. The naval patrol would be as follows:

The North Coast	Great Britain
Cape Busto to Portugal	France
Portugal to Cape de Gata	Great Britain
C. de Gata to C. Oropesa	Germany
C. Oropesa to France	Italy

France was also responsible for the coast of Spanish Morocco, Ibiza, and Majorca, whilst Italy patrolled Minorca. The plan was to be run by an International Board. Final agreement was reached on 8 March and six weeks later all was ready.

It was not long before incidents occurred, the most serious being the bombing of the German battleship the *Deutschland* whilst at anchor at Ibiza. Thirty-one sailors died as a result. As a reprisal for what was in fact a perfectly legal raid on an enemy base the Germans shelled Almería and threatened to withdraw from the patrol. Then the confusion was increased when Prieto suggested to his colleagues in Valencia that the German patrol fleet be bombed as a counter reprisal. Whilst Negrín was thinking this over the Communists informed Stalin of the suggestion. His answer was quite clear. There was to be no bombing and if Prieto persisted he was to be liquidated. The subject of Almería was quickly dropped. But the Communists did not forget Prieto. He in his turn began to start work on the task of loosening their hold on key positions in the armed forces. The fight between them was on.

One other major world power had no direct connection with the arrangements being made by the European countries – that power was the United States. Both the Republicans and the Democrats were neutral in outlook and Congress had passed a

Neutrality Act in 1935 which forbade all supply of arms to belligerents in a state of war as declared by the American President. The Spanish conflict was of course a civil war, but the Administration applied the 1935 Act to it, so Secretary of State Cordell Hull kept to a strictly impartial line. His position was in favour of a firm adherence to the non-intervention idea, so that any attempts to supply arms to either side were frowned upon. The semi-official embargo thus imposed was due to end on 28 December 1936. On that day the Vimalert Company got a licence to export aero engines to Republican Spain, but the Company's agent, Robert Cuse, at once began to transfer the engines to a Spanish ship, the *Mar Cantábrico*, just in case. His suspicions were justified for on 6 January 1937 both Houses of Congress had resolutions introduced giving the embargo the full force of law. The resolutions were passed but did not become effective until 8 January, so by sailing at once the *Mar Cantábrico* escaped. After a number of adventures, she reached the Bay of Biscay only to be seized by the Nationalists, some of her cargo being usefully employed against the Basques. An attempt to reverse the embargo decision failed in May 1938 when Roosevelt personally intervened to maintain it. However, in 1939 the President admitted that it had been a mistake and against international law. But it was too late to put the clock back then.

At least the American embargo was effective. Back in Europe in the summer of 1937 the European Control Plan was still in a state of suspension. An attempt by Lord Plymouth to revive control in a new form without naval patrols ran into trouble, with Count Dino Grandi of Italy being the main obstacle. When Neville Chamberlain became Prime Minister in June 1937, Anthony Eden thought that he would be in agreement with all the efforts being made by Britain to restore control. But on 29 July Chamberlain approached Mussolini privately with a view to improving relations, a move which culminated in the Anglo-Italian Mediterranean Pact signed on 16 April

100 H.M.S. *Resolution* arriving in the Tagus with the British Control Commission on board with orders to watch the Spanish-Portuguese frontier and prevent volunteers from entering Spain

1938 in which no objection was made to Italy retaining her troops in Spain until the Civil War ended. In his desire to 'improve relations' Chamberlain had effectively reduced the Non-Intervention Committee to a mere façade. What had been a more or less useful method of limiting the war, became an almost cynical sham when Britain failed to denounce publicly the various contraventions which both sides committed. She relied too much on paper promises and her statesmen only learned by hard experience the real worth of such agreements.

One of the subsidiary problems of non-intervention was that of the volunteers in Spain. These ranged from professionals seconded to either side, through full military formations, to individuals who came to help either as fighters or supporters. In August 1936 the German Foreign Minister von Neurath had suggested the banning of all volunteers whilst Hitler was agreeing to send men to Spain. On 24 December the British and French ambassadors to Germany, Italy, and Russia made representations about imposing such a ban. Russia was in support, so was Germany, and Italy did not object. Apparently the two latter powers agreed to support the plan publicly as they both thought General Franco had now received all he needed to win the war. So by early March numbers of volunteers found their way to Spain barred as all the countries of the Non-Intervention Committee now had laws prohibiting any volunteering at all. But although numbers were arrested, others managed to slip through, and Italy and Germany could still send men if needed, and in fact did so.

101   Three Republican cartoons by Allorza from *La Vanguardia* Showing Franco being manipulated by foreign interests

102 American Medical Bureau ambulance; one of two
sent to Spain to help the Republican cause

At one point the volunteer problem became part of another. In November 1936 the Nationalists issued a statement to the effect that henceforth they would stop consignments of war supplies for Republican use, such action being extended to attacking any foreign ships found in enemy ports. As it stood, this was illegal under normal International Law as this was civil war, and the Nationalists had not been granted belligerent rights. Thus the legality of the intended blockade depended on international recognition of the conflict as full war. Most of the British Cabinet supported such a grant, but Anthony Eden did not, largely because he did not wish to fall out with the French, who had vigorously opposed the idea. Eden won his battle so the rights were still not granted, British ships being ordered not to carry arms, only normal commercial cargoes. The same problem came up again on 6 April 1937 when the Nationalists declared a blockade of the northern ports to prevent arms and food getting to the Republicans. British merchant vessels could ask for and obtain Royal Navy protection up to the 3 mile limit but not beyond. If belligerent rights were granted, the belligerent could stop and search any suspect vessel on the high seas. Eventually British ships did get through and no further attempt was made to stop them going to Bilbao.

The next stage began in October 1937 when the question of granting belligerent rights was made dependent on the withdrawal of some of the volunteers under a new British plan. The Non-Intervention Sub-Committee dealing with such questions met on 16 October and the plan was studied and argued over for about two weeks before being agreed to on 4 November. It was then forwarded to the prospective belligerents. General Franco replied on 20 November, accepting the idea in general and giving a figure of 3,000 volunteers to be sent home as his contribution (this total being the precise number of sick or otherwise unfit Italians already sent home!). The Republicans followed suit on 1 December. They thought that the plan might lead to a break in the fighting and even to peace; if it did not it would give a breathing space which would

103   Marshal Goering (*right*) greeting General Aranda on behalf of the Führer, before presenting decorations to the Condor Legion

104   American Relief Ship poster, part of the campaign in America to raise money for the Republican refugees

allow time for reorganizing the army. Nothing happened for the moment, but when the plan came up again in February 1938, Eden tried to make withdrawal of volunteers an essential step before any discussions on Anglo-Italian agreement. Count Grandi refused to deal with the volunteer question apart from other discussions. Chamberlain agreed with this view so Eden resigned on 20 February. He had failed to make Chamberlain stand firm on a matter which he considered one of principle. A further attempt was made to revive the scheme in 1938, when the Russians agreed to it on 27 June, but once more nothing concrete resulted.

Strangely enough, the first really effective move arose from the Munich Agreement of September 1938. Russia now saw that her plan to create an alliance with France and Britain to counter Hitler was leading nowhere, so she began to cut down her own advisers in Spain and also her pro-Republican propaganda, changing her policy to one of friendship with Germany. The result was the withdrawal of the International Brigades from Spain, as Russia could not support them through the Comintern whilst she was moving towards a *rapprochement* with Hitler. The actual proposal for the withdrawal was made by Prime Minister Negrín before the League of Nations which was asked to make the arrangements. It was agreed to send a commission to Spain for this purpose. Events moved fast and all volunteers still in the great Ebro battle going on at this period were withdrawn. A parade was held on 15 November and by 15 January 1939 it was reported that 4,640 had left, 6,000 remaining in Catalonia where they were trapped shortly afterwards in the Nationalist advance.

Also during the Munich Conference a further step was taken when Mussolini promised Chamberlain that he would recall 10,000 Italian volunteers to help on the current Anglo-Italian negotiations. He actually left well over 15,000 men in Spain but his gesture was not an empty one. The 10,000 were withdrawn, reaching Naples on 10 October 1938. That was the end of the withdrawals during the war, the Condor Legion and the rest of the Italians departing after the final collapse at the end of May 1939.

The whole field of non-intervention and intervention continually presented new problems to the politicians involved. The story of the various moves in the long-drawn-out negotiations is often a tedious and repetitive one, not made any easier to follow by the vagueness of some proposals and the complex manœuvring behind the objections put forward to counter them. At times the whole affair seems to resemble a fantastic game of chess in which the rules change as the players make each move. It is not surprising that after months of negotiation the usually patient Anthony Eden could say that even his patience was well-nigh exhausted.

105   Front-page picture from the Italian newspaper *Corriere della Sera* of August 1938 showing Generals Dávila, Franco and Berti. It was proof such as this that made the Non-Intervention Committee seem so ineffectual

Nella zona di operazioni, in Spagna. - Da sinistra: il generale Davila, il generalissimo Franco, il generale Berti e un ufficiale di Stato Maggiore legionario

12 Offensive and Counter-Offensive – Teruel and Aragón

DURING THE PERIOD from the middle of October to the middle of December 1937, both sides had an opportunity to complete the task of remoulding or reorganizing their armies, both of which were now about the half-million mark in effective strength. There was also time to plan the next move or to prepare to meet that of the enemy. On the Nationalist side the prevailing opinion was that a further attempt to take or at least to encircle Madrid was the best step, as Catalonia was thought to be too likely to resist violently any attack from the Aragón front. But this assessment was a faulty reading of the military situation as events were subsequently to prove. The plan was developed for another drive on Madrid through Guadalajara – it was betrayed and once more the Republicans decided on a diversion. This time they would strike first.

The military map of Spain in the autumn of 1937 shows up one key area which could be the effective sector for an attack which would cause considerable problems for the Nationalists and which, if the offensive was successful, would be militarily beneficial to the Republic. Almost the only obvious choice is the Teruel salient, so that was selected as the next theatre of operations. The possible capture of this town had become something of an obsession with the troops facing it, so Negrín and his Minister of War, Prieto, decided to make the capture of Teruel a purely Spanish campaign. The International Brigades were not included in the forces earmarked for the attack. These were the XVIIIth, XXth, and XXIInd Army Corps commanded respectively by Heredia, Menéndez, and Ibarrola. The actual offensive against Teruel would be under the overall command of Hernández Sarabia, the opening attack being entrusted to the 11th Division under Lister. If Teruel fell and the salient could be reduced, the Republican lines between the centre and coast would be shorter and safer. If the advance could be pushed further, the road to Saragossa would be threatened. Much depended on the weather, as Teruel is the coldest place in Spain in winter and the region is one of the bleakest. Should there be a severe drop in temperature or a blizzard, the outcome of the offensive would be in the balance. All tank and lorry engines would freeze up, visibility would be minimal, and it would be impossible to dig trenches in the iron hard ground. Teruel would need to be captured quickly and a firm line established as far west as possible without delay before further advances could be safely undertaken.

On 15 December the 11th Division swung into action together with XVIIIth Corps, surrounding Teruel and taking the high ground to the west. The garrison commander, Colonel Rey d'Harcourt, then concentrated all his troops and civilian supporters in the southern half of the town. Barcelona Radio optimistically broadcast news of its capture two weeks too early. Meanwhile, the little garrison was ordered to hold on as relief was coming. On 29 December General Varela and General Aranda began the first of the Nationalist counter-offensives, backed by artillery and the German Condor Legion. They got to the high ground overlooking Teruel on 30 December, but a blizzard then defeated their attempt to get in. The battle stopped

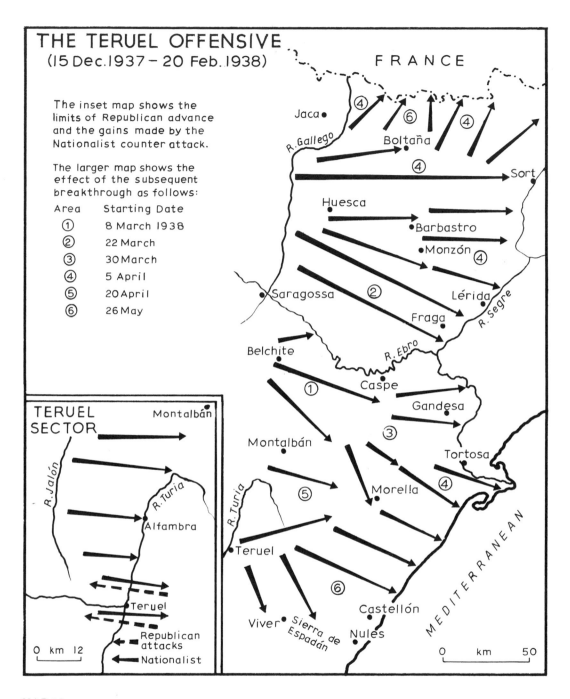

THE TERUEL OFFENSIVE
(15 Dec. 1937 – 20 Feb. 1938)

The inset map shows the
limits of Republican advance
and the gains made by the
Nationalist counter attack.

The larger map shows the
effect of the subsequent
breakthrough as follows:

Area	Starting Date
①	8 March 1938
②	22 March
③	30 March
④	5 April
⑤	20 April
⑥	26 May

FRANCE

Jaca
R. Gallego
Boltaña
Sort
Huesca
Barbastro
Monzón
Saragossa
Lérida
R. Segre
Fraga
R. Ebro
Belchite
Caspe
Gandesa
Montalbán
Tortosa
Morella
R. Turia
Teruel
MEDITERRANEAN
Castellón
Viver
Sierra de Espadán
Nules

TERUEL SECTOR

R. Jalón
R. Turia
Alfambra
Teruel

- - - Republican attacks
—— Nationalist

0 km 12

0 km 50

MAP 13

THE TERUEL OFFENSIVE. The attack on Teruel began on 15 December 1937. Appalling
weather halted the Nationalist relief forces and the town fell on 8 January 1938. It was re-
captured on 21 February. After a pause the Nationalists moved on to the Mediterranean, but
a thrust at Valencia was halted. Simultaneously the Aragón front became active. By 20 April
1938 the line ran from just east of Andorra to the Ebro delta through Lérida

105

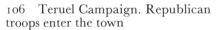
106   Teruel Campaign. Republican
troops enter the town

107   Loading bombs in an Italian
machine on the Ebro front

under the effect of deep snow and intense cold. No transport could move nor could either side see its targets or its enemy. In Teruel the struggle continued, the various garrison strongpoints being reduced one by one until on 8 January 1938, Colonel Rey d'Harcourt surrendered and the civilians trapped in the town were evacuated. Now the tables were turned – the besiegers became the besieged. To help reverse the deteriorating situation some of the International Brigades were ordered to the front, whilst the Nationalists waited for the weather to improve.

The second counter-offensive began on 17 January, taking the now usual form of heavy bombardment and an encircling movement. The Republican lines began to collapse, so the International Brigades on reserve were thrown in. The retreat still went on, though more slowly. An attempt was made to lessen the pressure by counter-attacks to the north. Teruel was still holding on.

A week later on 7 February a new threat appeared, this time to the north of the key sector where Generals Monasterio, Yagüe, and Aranda broke through to the river at Alfambra taking 7,000 prisoners of war and a large haul of vital supplies. This area then became the base for the fourth attack when Yagüe got over the river and swung south on 17 February. This was the first part of an encircling movement which nearly cut the town off three days later. Withdrawal was ordered so that most of the Republican troops escaped, leaving 10,000 dead in the town and a total of 14,000 prisoners in Nationalist hands. Prieto's hoped for victory had turned into a disastrous defeat. The Communist attack on him now came out into the open, with the result that Negrín had to transfer him from the War Ministry at the end of March 1938.

The hammering suffered by the Republican army at Teruel now presented General Franco with an unexpected opportunity to inflict a further defeat. He had sufficient strength in reserve to follow up a favourable situation fairly quickly, so in just over a month what can be termed the second part of the Teruel fighting began. General Dávila was put in command of IVth Army Corps and an Italian group under General Berti was added to this force. There were also two reserve divisions available in addition to the Condor Legion. General Varela, now in position east of Teruel, was ready to pounce with the Army of Castile if the moment came. The new offensive opened on 9 March in the Belchite sector. By 19 July the Nationalist line had reached the Mediterranean on a 70 kilometre front and ran north to the Pyrenees through Lérida. Perhaps Catalonia was not going to be such a difficult obstacle after all.

The first attacks met sharp resistance only in a few places. The defenders had had no time to recover from Teruel and weapons were in short supply. There was little co-ordination. By 22 March this advance had reached Caspe whilst the Republicans made desperate efforts to form a defensive line that would hold. Next a further advance began to the north on the Huesca-Saragossa sector, reaching Fraga on 30 March. The attack was then switched once more so that in five days further territory had been taken and the Nationalist salient now ran between Gandesa and Morella. Up to now the only really stiff opposition had been at Lérida where El Campesino had blocked the invaders for about a week, though the International Brigades had been able to slow down some of the columns, particularly at Gandesa, so that guns and supplies could be got away.

The advance continued in spite of all efforts, the territorial gains in the next push being considerable. The Jaca sector had taken up the move forward so that by 20 April the line had been straightened from Lérida through Sort to the Pyrenees apart from a small pocket north of Boltaña. At the same time Aranda and the Italians had pushed on just south of Gandesa to the sea. A drive forward north of Teruel then began, to be followed on 26 May by another drive from the Teruel sector itself which brought an extension of the coast line to just north of Sagunto, whilst the Pyrenean pocket was cleared. The main resistance in this final stage of the campaign had been offered by General Menéndez. As a result it took Aranda nearly a week to capture Castellón.

It was General Menéndez who now blocked the next stage in the offensive. The Nationalist objective was Valencia, but in this move their army ran into trouble. The

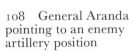

108   General Aranda pointing to an enemy artillery position

initial advance began on 5 July and made some progress until it reached the Sierra de Espadán, a formidable barrier which runs almost to the sea. The Republican defenders held their positions in the hills for a month. Then the key position of Sarrión was stormed and the whole front collapsed again. The Nationalists began to renew their advance at speed. Then they ran up against the last defence line covering Valencia, a well-built trench system running from the coast into the Sierra. Shelling, bombing, and infantry attacks failed to have any effect so by the end of July the attempt to break through ceased in face of the heavy casualties being suffered. Republican Spain had been cut in two, she had suffered heavy losses in men and material, but she still had the capacity to hit back hard. The war was not yet over.

The danger to Valencia had thus been averted for the time being, but it was clear to Negrín and his War Council that their enemy would try again. Once more the idea of a diversionary offensive was taken up towards the end of July 1938 when General Rojo, the Chief of Staff, put forward a plan to launch an attack across the river Ebro on a wide front in the Gandesa sector. If surprise was achieved and all went well, it could become possible to reopen communications with central Spain. If the campaign failed, the defeat at Teruel had shown clearly what would then happen.

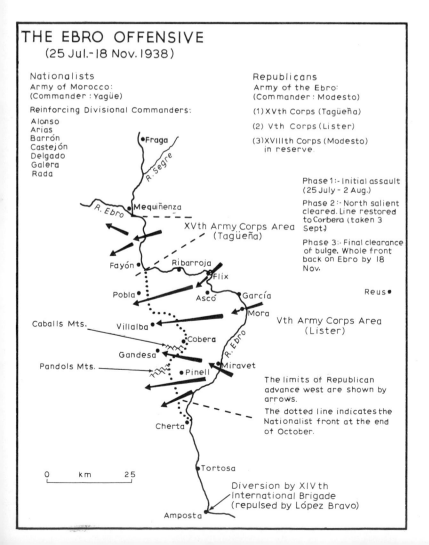

THE EBRO OFFENSIVE
(25 Jul.-18 Nov. 1938)

Nationalists
Army of Morocco:
(Commander : Yagüe)

Reinforcing Divisional Commanders:
Alonso
Arias
Barrón
Castejón
Delgado
Galera
Rada

Republicans
Army of the Ebro:
(Commander : Modesto)

(1) XVth Corps (Tagüeña)

(2) Vth Corps (Lister)

(3) XVIIIth Corps (Modesto)
in reserve.

Phase 1:- Initial assault
(25 July - 2 Aug.)

Phase 2:- North salient
cleared. Line restored
to Corbera (taken 3
Sept.)

Phase 3:- Final clearance
of bulge. Whole front
back on Ebro by 18
Nov.

The limits of Republican
advance west are shown by
arrows.

The dotted line indicates the
Nationalist front at the end
of October.

•Fraga
R. Segre
R. Ebro
•Mequiñenza
XVth Army Corps Area
(Tagüeña)
Fayón •
Ribarroja
•Flix
Pobla •
Ascó
•García
Reus•
Caballs Mts.
Villalba •
•Mora
Vth Army Corps Area
(Lister)
•Cobera
R. Ebro
Gandesa•
Pandols Mts.
•Miravet
•Pinell
Cherta•
•Tortosa

0   km   25

Diversion by XIVth
International Brigade
(repulsed by López Bravo)
Amposta•

MAP 14
THE EBRO OFFENSIVE.
The last Republican
diversionary campaign
began on 25 July 1938
under Modesto with three
army corps crossing the
Ebro in the Gandesa
sector. Gandesa was
reached but not taken,
and under the heavy
pressure of Nationalist
attacks the ground lost
was recovered by 18
November

109 Aragón front. Troops under winter conditions

The plan was accepted even though reserves of war material were low and the French frontier, which had been open for a short time, was now closed again so no supplies could be expected by that route. Three Army Corps were allocated to the offensive, the Vth under Lister, the XVth under Manuel Tagüeña, and the XVIIIth in reserve under the control of the Supreme Commander Modesto. There was adequate artillery support but few anti-aircraft guns. Crossings were to be made at three places, one between Mequiñenza at the junction of the Ebro and the Segre and Fayón downstream, the second between Fayón and Cherta, and the third 50 kilometres nearer the sea at Amposta. Shortly after midnight on 24–25 July, XVth Corps crossed successfully at the first point, whilst Lister's Vth Corps crossed at several places in the second sector, and also managed to get over the river at Amposta. The initial crossings were by boat, then pontoon bridges were put into position for tanks, guns, and further infantry. Initial surprise was complete, only the Amposta attack being defeated. In the centre sector Lister was busy destroying the defences of Colonel Peñarredonda, the Nationalist commander of the area in front of Gandesa. By the end of the day, he had got to within sight of Gandesa and had secured all the higher ground.

As at Teruel, the Nationalist reaction was swift, with seven divisions being sent to stem the advance. The battle for Gandesa was fierce, Republican casualties grew, and by 2 August the front was stabilized. The gamble had failed. The attackers began to dig in to face intensive air bombardment. Any man retreating without specific orders was to be shot. The Nationalists then brought the full force of their artillery to bear using their infantry in small groups in limited counter-attacks. By 7 August the northernmost bridgehead had been cleared. Then on 11 August the high ground known as the Sierra de Pandols to the south of Gandesa was attacked and partially cleared. General Yagüe then took the neighbouring Monte Gaeta. On 3 September a larger scale thrust captured Corbera at the end of the Sierra de Caballs in front of Gandesa. The Nationalists' complete command of the air space above the battlefield and the weight of their artillery fire began to tell; the initial uplift to Republican morale began to give way to anxiety. Morale in the Nationalist zone was no better as the toughness of the Republican resistance became known.

However, the situation slowly began to change in favour of the Nationalists. Stalin had become convinced that he would never get any alliance with France and Britain against Germany, so had redirected his policy to an understanding with Germany. This meant that he could no longer keep the International Brigades in Spain to fight an ally of the power with which he was aiming to come to terms. Accordingly this force was withdrawn, their last battle being on 22 September. Meanwhile General Franco was patiently working on the plan for his main counter-attack. This began on 20 October on a very limited front in the Sierra de Caballs.

Within twenty-four hours the Sierra had been cleared by a combination of furious artillery fire and heavy infantry attack. The Nationalists now commanded the whole battle area. Next day their right flank also cleared the remaining positions on the Sierra de Pandols and reached the Ebro. Armour and infantry were thrusting deep into the Republican lines but a complete rout was prevented by a brilliant fighting retreat by Lister who covered the withdrawing Republican troops with great skill. By 18 November the Ebro offensive was over, and once more the Republic had seen its initial success turned into tragic defeat with 30,000 dead, the loss of some 200 planes and a large quantity of weapons of all kinds. It seemed that nothing that her armies undertook was ever to be wholly successful – and now half a million enemy troops were preparing to follow up their latest victory. The next objective now was clearly going to be Catalonia.

110 Soldier using a trench periscope

111 The Ebro offensive. Typical scene in a field hospital, where facilities were often extremely makeshift. The doctor is giving a blood transfusion

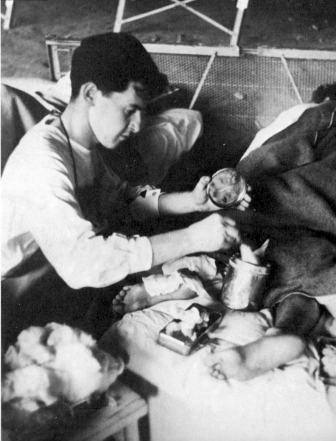

13 Unity is Strength

THE LONGER A WAR CONTINUES one basic problem becomes more and more pressing. War weariness and the effects of continuous tension must not be permitted to bring about a weakening of the will to resist. The danger that such a lowering of morale might occur had to be faced by the leaders of both sides in the Civil War, though it was more likely to happen in the Republican zone as the strenuous efforts to stop the Nationalist advance led to successive defeats. One of the reasons for continued resistance in that zone was to be found in the dynamic personality of the Prime Minister from 1937 onwards. Whilst President Azaña seemed to fade more and more into the background, Dr Negrín developed into a real leader.

When Negrín had come to power in May 1937, he had done so largely by making use of the Communists' hatred of Largo Caballero. He himself was a Socialist of moderate views but he also had the political skill to keep himself relatively free from outside control whilst benefiting by the efficiency of men whom he disliked. He was essentially a planner determined to win the war, but he was also determined to remain independent. Hence the Communists found that their attempts to increase their influence were only partly successful even when the weakened power of the Anarchists and the destruction of the Partido Obrero de Unión Marxista (P.O.U.M.) gave them an ideal opportunity to expand. Their lengthy attempts to create a unified group with the Socialists actually reached the stage of a concrete agreement in August 1937, but two months later unification was still no nearer. Then Negrín intervened to stop the negotiations – he had no wish to see the Socialists come under Communist domination. Meanwhile his Minister of War, Indalecio Prieto, was now ready to start work on reducing the political strength of the Communists, largely by forbidding officers to indulge in political activity and by cutting down the number of Commissars.

The basic aim of Negrín and his Cabinet was thus to ensure a balance between parties so that the government would always have some control. The Communists were in a dilemma in the autumn of 1937 as a consequence. At the meeting of the Cortes, held in October, they proposed that new elections should be held on the grounds that their present sixteen members was too small a total as they now had over 300,000 party members. Negrín rejected the proposal, quite naturally. The Communist problem now was whether they should leave the government or accept the rebuff and stay on. They stayed.

It was not long before they succeeded in converting one of Prieto's plans to their own advantage. An essential activity of war is counter-intelligence work aimed at detecting spying, sabotage, and like enemy attempts at disruption. In Republican Spain the Russian Orlov had his own group, but in addition there were several other agencies which overlapped. Prieto hoped to bring all these services under one control by setting up the Servicio de Investigación Militar (S.I.M.), which was to be run by someone he could trust. After some difficulty he appointed Colonel Uribarri as the head. This officer was a Socialist and firmly loyal to Prieto, but before long his organization had been infiltrated and had been converted to a Communist service on the lines of Orlov's with its use of torture. Negrín seems to have been unaware of what had

112   Bomb damage scene in Barcelona in January 1938.
A few seconds after the photo was taken everyone in it was
killed by a further bomb

happened for some time, but when he did discover the truth, it was too late for him to do anything. The Communists now possessed a means of dealing with their enemies as well as spies, a means which they could use in conjunction with the new Military Tribunals which replaced the former Popular Tribunals in 1938. A report from S.I.M. was adequate evidence for a conviction.

The most important material problem at this time was food production. The Negrín Government tried to improve output by reducing the number of collectives which did not always supply their surplus produce for use elsewhere. But the chief difficulty was the shortage of available labour so that harvests suffered, and little could be done. Madrid in particular was undergoing a certain amount of hardship which was to increase in 1938 to near starvation conditions. The temporary opening of the French frontier from November 1937 did something to keep essential foreign arms supplies flowing for a time.

By the end of 1937 Negrín had thus managed to give the appearance of unity to Republican Spain and to increase the strength of his own position. He had moved the seat of government to Barcelona from November 1937, which led to some friction with the Catalan government. But he had established himself in a commanding position over the Anarchists and Largo Caballero's Socialists. He had to be careful when handling the Communists, but even they with their superior organization were not having things all their own way by any means.

In the spring of 1938 the Communists managed to regain some of the ground they had lost by striking at the Prime Minister through Prieto, whose Teruel offensive had turned into such a defeat. The attack opened against the now despondent Minister of War in March but made little headway at the start. Prieto was now so depressed that he had tried to contact the Nationalists over the possibility of a negotiated peace settle-

113   Bomb damage in a Barcelona street in March 1938

ment. Negrín was then in France to see the new French Premier Blum, and when he returned he found morale at a low point. The Nationalist offensive in Aragón had reduced Prieto to complete demoralization. Negrín did his best to restore confidence and to protect Prieto, but by the end of March he had made up his mind to transfer his War Minister. Prieto refused any alternative post, thus leaving the Cabinet.

When the Nationalists cut Spain in two, the central government stayed in Barcelona and General Miaja was made the Supreme Commander of all the rest, soon to be given charge of civil administration as well. In general at this time the Communists still had considerable power in the army, particularly in the Army of the Ebro which was practically wholly led by their men. But there were numbers of other senior officers too who were Anarchists or Socialists. Further military supplies arrived in April and May 1938. The mood of defeatism had been overcome. On 1 May Negrín published a list of thirteen points as a statement of his government's aims, but also as an indication to the Nationalists of his basic terms for a negotiated peace. The international situation was gloomy and events seemed to be moving towards a general war. If this was a true assessment, there was more than a hope that the Spanish Civil War would have to end by an agreed settlement. But all Negrín's attempts to establish contact failed, and now the Russians were turning lukewarm whilst the French had again closed the frontier on 13 June. To tighten up control, Negrín wanted to introduce militarization of the Military Tribunals, of port control, and nationalization of the arms industry. This provoked a Cabinet crisis. Negrín seems to have become depressed at the continued struggle at this time and thought of retiring in favour of Companys. But the mood passed quickly. He reorganized his Cabinet and began again the task of trying to make peace – again without success in spite of a secret meeting in Switzerland with a German official.

The failure of the Ebro offensive and Russia's change of policy added to Negrín's problems. The shortage of food was now becoming acute in spite of international aid. Industrial output began to fall. The Nationalists swept into Catalonia. The Republic began to disintegrate though Negrín was still making brave efforts to hold things together. Surrender was inevitable. Negrín and his ministers left for France. The war was over.

The Spanish Civil War is remarkable for the number of men who, though of humble origins or without any experience of war and politics, rose to be outstanding leaders. Dr Negrín, by profession a biologist, would never have thought of becoming a politician in normal circumstances. But in the stress of war he showed he possessed the right qualities for the toughest job of all in Republican Spain, that of Prime Minister. His astuteness and intelligence enabled him to keep at least partial control over the groups and parties seeking to dominate. The Communists were always a source of division and he was forced to temporize to avoid the danger of internal strife. But overall he did a quite remarkable job in preventing the Republican zone from falling apart into warring factions for so long.

Nationalist Spain was much more obviously based on the military attitude to ruling, its organization being almost completely directed towards the prosecution of the war. Social developments or political programmes were thus of little importance, and only organizations such as Auxilio Social and its various subsidiaries flourished, these being of course essential complements to the war effort. Firm control of the zone was maintained, this being formalized from February 1937 by trial by courts martial and by official expropriation committees. On the economic side, Nationalist Spain showed greater stability too with a strong peseta, ample food supplies, and good credit facilities. There was also a much firmer central control of the armed forces with some attempt to build up production for war needs. As has been noted already, the rise of General Franco to be Head of State, Supreme Commander, and Head of the Falange gave the Nationalist zone a greater stability in spite of disagreements under the surface. General Jordana was in charge of the administrative *junta* at Burgos, whilst Serrano Suñer was occupied in creating a political philosophy for the new state.

The next major development was the setting up of a forty-eight member National Council which was an advisory body only. This came into being on 2 December 1937, all its members being nominees of General Franco and being chosen from all the varied groups still in existence. Backing the leaders at this time was a largely enthusiastic middle class, although the zone did contain quite a number of potential troublemakers still. But life was not too hard – food was plentiful as was fuel. Bullfights had begun again, and cafés and cinemas were doing well. Prices had only risen slightly. Education had once more regained its former religious background as the church came back more and more into the picture. Even the apparently flamboyant Queipo de Llano was hard

114 [*opposite*] Bomb-damage scene in a Barcelona street in March 1938

115 A ten céntimos postage stamp used to make a cardboard 'coin' in the Republican zone, as there was a shortage of suitable metal. On the back is printed the coat of arms of the Republic

at work developing the agriculture and industry of the south. To ensure the strength of the armed forces, conscription had been introduced for all men between the ages of eighteen and twenty-nine. Similarly, to keep the social services effective, women were also conscripted between seventeen and twenty-five if not already doing essential work. The government of Nationalist Spain was very much a military government of a traditional and conservative pattern.

The combination of *junta* and National Council developed into a form closer to the normal system of a modern state by the end of January 1938, when a Cabinet was formed. General Franco was the President of the Council, whilst General Jordana now held the office of Vice-President and was also the Foreign Minister. The other members comprised two more generals, a number of technocrats, and representatives of the Falange, a Monarchist, a Carlist, and the now powerful Serrano Suñer who was Minister of the Interior as well as Secretary-General of the Falange. There was no place for General Queipo de Llano, who made at least one injudicious statement to the effect that as a true patriot he supported General Franco who was the man with a solution for Spain's present troubles, but should the General falter he would attack him just as he had risen against the Republic. It was never wise to make public criticisms of the Caudillo. In disgust at his omission, Queipo de Llano ceased his famous nightly broadcasts.

As 1938 passed the new ministers began to lay down the lines along which the state they hoped to create after the war would develop. By mid-March they had finally worked out a Labour Charter which covered such matters as a minimum wage, allowances, hours of work, and so on. There were to be five sections or chambers covering agriculture, commerce including industry, public service, shipping, and culture in general. Within each section there were to be a chain of syndicates rising from district corporations up to the top. The state shortly afterwards took over control of the press and laid down regulations for the employment and pay of all journalists. Full state control was clearly going to be the guiding principle in future in Spain.

The apparent solidity of the system being created was not yet proof against every contingency. The slowing down of the offensive which developed after the Teruel victory led to Falangist criticism of the way General Franco was conducting the war. This military failure led to a drop in morale in general by the middle of 1938. The halting of the Valencia attack and the opening success of the Ebro offensive in July added to the despondency so that there were signs of defeatist quarrels. But even though things were going badly General Franco held to his course, the counter-offensive began as planned, and there was no question of a mediated peace or a negotiated settlement.

Some of his generals might have other ideas, the Falangists might be restive, but his sole aim was the total surrender of the Republicans.

The success of the counter-offensive restored confidence to some extent, though by the autumn of 1938 conditions of living were worsening. Prices were now rising whilst wages were not. Industry was producing for the war effort so there was little to buy in the shops. The Christmas of 1938 was not a cheerful one unless one had money. Then came the fall of Catalonia, the *rapprochement* with France, and on 27 February 1939 recognition by both France and Great Britain. As the Republic began to fall apart all that General Franco needed to do was to wait. The unity which he had succeeded in imposing, his patience and refusal to act hurriedly, his singleness of purpose, all these had given him final victory at long last.

116   General Franco taking the salute at the Victory Parade in 1938

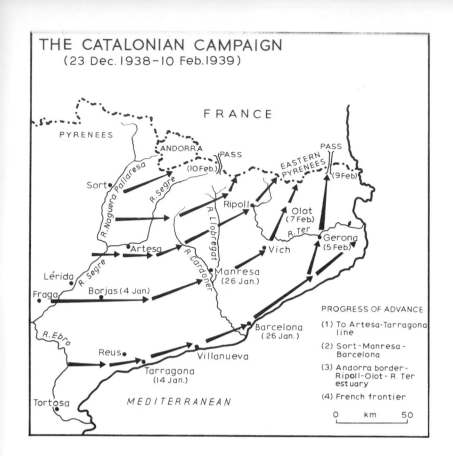

THE CATALONIAN CAMPAIGN
(23 Dec.1938–10 Feb.1939)

FRANCE

PYRENEES

ANDORRA

PASS
(10 Feb.)

EASTERN
PYRENEES

PASS
(9 Feb.)

Sort

R. Naguera Pallaresa

R. Segre

R. Llobregat

Ripoll

Olot
(7 Feb.)

R. Ter

Gerona
(5 Feb.)

Artesa

R. Segre

R. Cardoner

Vich

Lérida

Manresa
(26 Jan.)

Fraga

Borjas (4 Jan.)

R. Ebro

Barcelona
(26 Jan.)

Reus

Villanueva

PROGRESS OF ADVANCE

(1) To Artesa-Tarragona
line

(2) Sort-Manresa-
Barcelona

(3) Andorra border-
Ripoll-Olot-R. Ter
estuary

(4) French frontier

Tarragona
(14 Jan.)

Tortosa

MEDITERRANEAN

0   km   50

MAP 15
THE CATALONIAN
CAMPAIGN. The capture
of Catalonia took six
weeks with six armies of
Spanish and Italian
troops in the field. The
campaign began near
Lérida on 23 December
1938, only one or two
sectors offering serious
resistance. Barcelona fell
on 26 January 1939.
Two days later some
half a million civilians
and soldiers crossed into
France as refugees. By
10 February the whole
area had been occupied

117   Catalan Campaign.
French police controlling
a crowd of refugees at the
Le Perthus entry point
into France

14 The Fall of Catalonia

BY THE LATE AUTUMN of 1938 the Republicans were facing a most dangerous situation with a direct threat now poised at Catalonia. But General Rojo, the Chief of Staff, estimated that the enemy could not hope to mount an offensive for some months. He was apparently unaware of the fresh military supplies sent in by Germany, and he certainly underestimated the efficiency of the Nationalist military machine. Perhaps he relied too much on the size of the forces defending Catalonia which amounted to nearly a quarter of a million men under that able commander Hernández Sarabia. His failure to judge the position correctly was fatal – Catalonia was overrun in six weeks.

On the other side, the Nationalists had moved six armies into position, the line being as follows from north to south: Army Corps of Urgel (Muñoz Grandes), Army of the Maestrazgo (García Valiño), four Italian divisions (Gambara), Army of Navarra (Solchaga), Army of Morocco (Yagüe). Catalonia was to be attacked by 300,000 troops. After two postponements the date for the offensive was fixed for 23 December.

The initial assault was made south of Lérida and broke through at once. The same thing happened at the north end so the whole line of the river Segre collapsed. To stem the drive the Vth Army Corps under Lister was thrown in with the result that he held up the attack for about a fortnight. But he could not withstand the constant armoured attacks so the Italians drove him out of his positions on 3 January 1939. East of Lérida Borjas Blancas fell on 4 January and the advance was on. Tarragona was captured on 14 January, all efforts to stop or slow down the Nationalist columns failed. Refugees poured into Barcelona where they suffered all the terrors of air raids. The French government authorized the reopening of the frontier to allow war supplies through but it was too late. After a short lull, the advance began again.

On 24 January the river Llobregat was reached on a wide front and Manresa fell. The Republican government left Barcelona for Gerona. In the capital the situation was desperate with all will to resist gone. On 26 January the Nationalists were close to the city on the north and west sides. They entered it at noon as half a million people fled north to the frontier, where vast crowds of hungry and terrified men, women, and children gathered, not knowing what was to happen to them. The French government was forced to open the frontier to them, and on 28 January the first civilians were allowed through. Nearly a quarter of a million passed into France. Then on 5 February the French authorities allowed troops in, and in the next five days another quarter of a million Spaniards came in. Women and children were quickly dispersed into other parts of the country, whilst those left were grouped in fifteen camps in primitive conditions. The task of dealing with such an influx of refugees was so complex that only the barest of necessities could be provided until other governments agreed to help.

Back in Catalonia, the advancing troops took Gerona on 5 February. Figueras was captured on 8 February and the frontier reached the next day. The whole frontier was occupied by the Nationalist forces on 10 February shortly after the last men of the Army of the Ebro had passed through to safety. The war in the east was over. With the help of Germany's last major contribution of arms, General Franco and his armies had captured a province and destroyed nearly one half of the Republic's effective armed forces. The autonomous state of Catalonia ceased to exist and Spanish replaced Catalan as the official language. The Generalitat was now past history.

15 The Final Act

SEVEN WEEKS WERE TO PASS before the end finally came on 31 March 1939. The situation in the Republican zone was now desperate everywhere. There were still nearly half a million men under arms, but there were acute shortages of weapons, ammunition, and planes. Food was very short and deaths by starvation increased. Hope had almost completely vanished. Negrín had reached Alicante with his Cabinet from Toulouse after a flight from Barcelona. But even he seemed undecided as to what course of action to take when he met his senior generals on 12 February. President Azaña now in Paris refused to return to Spain. Then General Franco issued a decree covering persons who had committed subversive activities or who had opposed the Nationalists actively or passively. As the period which the decree was intended to refer to ran from October 1934 to date, it gave extensive powers of punishment and execution to the victors. The apparently drastic nature of this act was later modified somewhat when General Franco assured Chamberlain that he was not intending to take reprisals, only to ensure a just peace.

The effect of these two official statements on the Republicans was two-fold. On one hand, the obvious intention behind the decree convinced Negrín that he could not ask for peace, so he came round to the Communist view that resistance would have to be continued. On the other hand, the apparent moderation of the telegram encouraged many non-Communist officers to think that an approach to General Franco by one of them would be successful. The upshot was in effect another civil war.

Colonel Segismundo Casado emerged as the leader of the group of anti-Communist officers. He was the officer commanding the Army of the Centre based in Madrid, and amongst his subordinate commanders was Colonel Cipriano Mera of the IVth Army Group who was to give him invaluable support. Casado began by banning the Communist paper *Mundo Obrero*. Negrín came to Madrid himself to see what was happening, but his interview with Casado led nowhere, although the Prime Minister agreed to Casado's offer to open peace negotiations himself. And peace was now an urgent matter with 400 people dying weekly in Madrid from starvation alone in spite of large quantities of foreign food coming into Spain.

On 26 February Negrín discussed the situation with his military leaders again. Opinions were divided but he seems to have felt that he had the support necessary to control Casado and took steps to this end. Meanwhile the Colonel approached various other officers explaining his plans and urging their support with some success. Attempts by Negrín to get him to come and visit him were met by excuses as Casado was certain these invitations were a trap.

Negrín then took action to prevent trouble at Cartagena naval base when Admiral Buiza seemed to be planning to join Casado. A reliable Communist, Colonel Galán, was sent there. The result was a rising in which Fifth Column Falangists joined. Buiza took his fleet to sea and made for French North Africa. The rising was put down when the 4th Division arrived to deal with the situation.

Back in Madrid Casado now took steps to defend himself if attacked with the help of one of Mera's brigades. He also assumed the position of President of a revolutionary *junta*, and when Negrín telephoned him shortly afterwards, he calmly informed the Prime Minister of his revolt. The position was such that the Russians now abandoned any further ideas of urging resistance and hurriedly left for home. Only the Spanish Communists took up the challenge. Casado's defence precautions were soon justified as the 8th Division under Major Ascanio moved towards Madrid on 8 March. Negrín and his Ministers still hoped to control the dangerous situation which was developing but their hopes were dashed when it became clear that Casado was gaining ground. They then flew to France.

Casado now came under attack from the Communists who penned him in the south-eastern part of the capital. But his friend Mera quickly moved to his relief so that on 8 March fighting broke out in Madrid itself with the Communists in control. They hesitated at the crucial moment so next day Mera succeeded in taking their headquarters whilst Casado broke out of his area. Eventually a cease fire was arranged. Casado was now free to begin negotiating with the Nationalists, one of whose agents had made an appearance in Madrid. He was a Colonel Centaño and he and Casado started discussions without much success, as the latter would not accept the demand for unconditional surrender. But on 19 March General Franco gave permission for negotiations to open whilst he made preparations for his armies to advance if need be. The negotiations broke down when the Republican air force failed to surrender on 25 March as arranged. An attempt by Casado to renew discussions was met by the reply that the Nationalist armies were about to move. Republican units wishing to surrender were to show white flags before the artillery bombardment began.

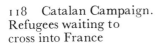
118   Catalan Campaign. Refugees waiting to cross into France

On 26 March the first move came when General Yagüe began advancing in the Sierra Morena area. There was no opposition as the Republican units abandoned their positions. Next day another column began moving from Toledo with the same result. The Army of the Centre surrendered under Casado's instructions whilst that officer flew to Valencia over long columns of troops going home or trying to get to the coast in search of ships. That same day, 27 March 1939, the Nationalists entered Madrid.

In Valencia and in all the coast towns of the area thousands of refugees and local people tried to escape by sea but only a few succeeded in doing so. The Falange took over Valencia, which was entered by the military on 30 March. The last towns left fell on 31 March when Almería, Murcia, and Cartagena were taken over. When General Franco was told of this, his reply was a typical: 'Muy bien, muchas gracias' (Very good, thank you very much). The war was over, the next task was the creation of the new Spain. The Caudillo was not the type of man to waste time on unnecessary speeches. There was work to be done, work that was going to occupy him for the rest of his life.

119   General Yagüe

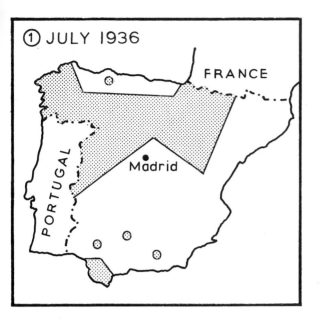

① JULY 1936

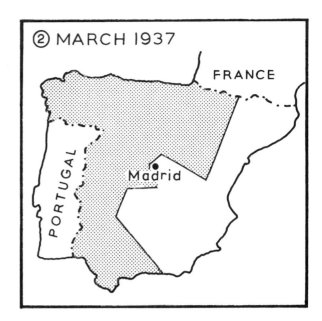

② MARCH 1937

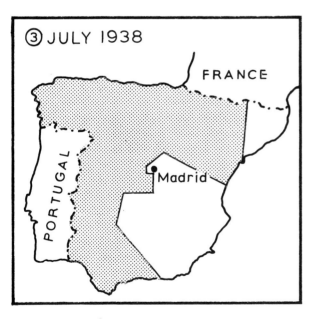

③ JULY 1938

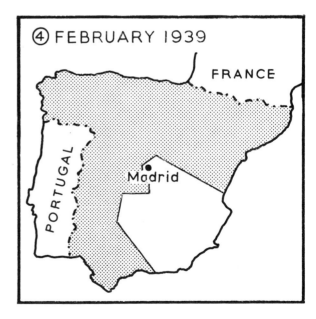

④ FEBRUARY 1939

MAP 16   THE MAIN STAGES OF NATIONALIST ADVANCE

ACKNOWLEDGEMENTS

THE AUTHOR and publishers wish to record their grateful thanks to copyright owners for the use of the following illustrations:

Camera Press Limited for: 54, 55, 91, 98, 108

Contemporary Films Limited for stills taken from *To Die in Madrid*; 60, 61, 62, 76, 77, 94

Eyre & Spottiswoode for photographs taken from *Franco, a biography*, by Brian Crozier; 18, 40, 43, 57

Foto Mas, Barcelona for: 16, 47

Genovés, Juan, for: 88

Mr A. Graham for: 86

The International Brigade for: 2, 19, 20, 51, 95, 96, 97, 98, 99, 105, 106, 111

Librería Editorial San Martín for: 64, 67, 71, 73, 79, 84, 109

Mansell Collection for: 9, 14, 15, 24, 26

Mary Evans Picture Library for: 8, 11, 13, 81, 101, 118

Museo del Prado for: 3

Museo Romántico for: 7

Ministerio de Información y Turismo for: 25

Museum of Modern Art, N.Y. for: 82

Neville Spearman Limited for photographs taken from *Combat over Spain* by the Duke of Lerma: 58, 83, 107

Paul Popper Limited for: 10, 17, 21, 27, 29, 30, 31, 36, 37, 38, 41, 44, 46, 50, 52, 53, 92, 100

Princeton University Press for: 28, 39, 45

Mr Ian Robertson for: 7

Radio Times Hulton Picture Library for: 4, 5, 12, 22, 23, 63, 117

Mr R. G. Shelley for: 1, 34, 35, 42, 48, 49, 56, 59, 65, 66, 68, 70, 72, 74, 75, 78, 80, 85, 87, 89, 90, 93, 102, 103, 104, 110, 112, 113, 114, 115, 116, 119

Servicio Informativo Español for: 32, 69

Index